Uncover 3 Combo A

Ben Goldstein · Ceri Jones
with Susan Banman Sileci

Student's Book

CAMBRIDGE UNIVERSITY PRESS

Discovery EDUCATION

CAMBRIDGE
UNIVERSITY PRESS

University Printing House, Cambridge CB2 8BS, United Kingdom

One Liberty Plaza, 20th Floor, New York, NY 10006, USA

477 Williamstown Road, Port Melbourne, VIC 3207, Australia

314–321, 3rd Floor, Plot 3, Splendor Forum, Jasola District Centre,
New Delhi – 110025, India

79 Anson Road, #06–04/06, Singapore 079906

Cambridge University Press is part of the University of Cambridge.

It furthers the University's mission by disseminating knowledge in the pursuit of education, learning and research at the highest international levels of excellence.

www.cambridge.org
Information on this title: www.cambridge.org/9781107515086

© Cambridge University Press 2015

This publication is in copyright. Subject to statutory exception
and to the provisions of relevant collective licensing agreements,
no reproduction of any part may take place without the written
permission of Cambridge University Press.

First published 2015

20 19 18 17 16 15 14 13 12 11 10

Printed in Great Britain by CPI Group (UK) Ltd, Croydon CR0 4YY

A catalog record for this publication is available from the British Library.

ISBN 978-1-107-49340-7 Student's Book 3
ISBN 978-1-107-49342-1 Student's Book with Online Workbook and Online Practice 3
ISBN 978-1-107-51508-6 Combo 3A
ISBN 978-1-107-51511-6 Combo 3B
ISBN 978-1-107-49347-6 Teacher's Book 3
ISBN 978-1-107-49345-2 Workbook with Online Practice 3
ISBN 978-1-107-49352-0 Presentation Plus Disc 3
ISBN 978-1-107-49348-3 Class Audio CDs (3) 3
ISBN 978-1-107-49350-6 Video DVD 3

Additional resources for this publication at www.cambridge.org/uncover

The publishers have no responsibility for the persistence or accuracy of URLs
for external or third-party Internet websites referred to in this publication, and
do not guarantee that any content on such websites is, or will remain, accurate
or appropriate. Information regarding prices, travel timetables, and other factual
information given in this work is correct at the time of first printing but the
publishers do not guarantee the accuracy of such information thereafter.

Art direction, book design, photo research, and layout services: QBS Learning
Audio production: John Marshall Media

Acknowledgments

Many teachers, coordinators, and educators shared their opinions, their ideas, and their experience to help create *Uncover*. The authors and publisher would like to thank the following people and their schools for their help in shaping the series.

In Mexico:

María Nieves Maldonado Ortiz (Colegio Enrique Rébsamen); Héctor Guzmán Pineda (Liceo Europeo); Alfredo Salas López (Campus Universitario Siglo XXI); Rosalba Millán Martínez (IIPAC [Instituto Torres Quintero A.C.]); Alejandra Rubí Reyes Badillo (ISAS [Instituto San Angel del Sur]); José Enrique Gutiérrez Escalante (Centro Escolar Zama); Gabriela Juárez Hernández (Instituto de Estudios Básicos Amado Nervo); Patricia Morelos Alonso (Instituto Cultural Ingles, S.C.); Martha Patricia Arzate Fernández, (Colegio Valladolid); Teresa González, Eva Marina Sánchez Vega (Colegio Salesiano); María Dolores León Ramírez de Arellano, (Liceo Emperadores Aztecas); Esperanza Medina Cruz (Centro Educativo Francisco Larroyo); Nubia Nelly Martínez García (Salesiano Domingo Savio); Diana Gabriela González Benítez (Colegio Ghandi); Juan Carlos Luna Olmedo (Centro Escolar Zama); Dulce María Pascual Granados (Esc. Juan Palomo Martínez); Roberto González, Fernanda Audirac (Real Life English Center); Rocio Licea (Escuela Fundación Mier y Pesado); Diana Pombo (Great Union Institute); Jacobo Cortés Vázquez (Instituto María P. de Alvarado); Michael John Pryor (Colegio Salesiano Anáhuac Chapalita)

In Brazil:

Renata Condi de Souza (Colégio Rio Branco); Sônia Maria Bernal Leites (Colégio Rio Branco); Élcio Souza (Centro Universitário Anhaguera de São Paulo); Patricia Helena Nero (Private teacher); Célia Elisa Alves de Magalhães (Colégio Cruzeiro-Jacarepaguá); Lilia Beatriz Freitas Gussem (Escola Parque-Gávea); Sandra Maki Kuchiki (Easy Way Idiomas); Lucia Maria Abrão Pereira Lima (Colégio Santa Cruz-São Paulo); Deborah de Castro Ferroz de Lima Pinto (Mundinho Segmento); Clara Vianna Prado (Private teacher); Ligia Maria Fernandes Diniz (Escola Internacional de Alphaville); Penha Aparecida Gaspar Rodrigues (Colégio Salesiano Santa Teresinha); Silvia Castelan (Colégio Santa Catarina de Sena); Marcelo D'Elia (The Kids Club Guarulhos); Malyina Kazue Ono Leal (Colégio Bandeirantes); Nelma de Mattos Santana Alves (Private teacher); Mariana Martins Machado (Britannia Cultural); Lilian Bluvol Vaisman (Curso Oxford); Marcelle Belfort Duarte (Cultura Inglesa-Duque de Caxias); Paulo Dantas (Britannia International English); Anauã Carmo Vilhena (York Language Institute); Michele Amorim Estellita (Lemec – Lassance Modern English Course); Aida Setton (Colégio Uirapuru); Maria Lucia Zaorob (CEL-LEP); Marisa Veiga Lobato (Interlíngua Idiomas); Maria Virgínia Lebrón (Independent consultant); Maria Luiza Carmo (Colégio Guilherme Dumont Villares/CEL-LEP); Lucia Lima (Independent consultant); Malyina Kazue Ono Leal (Colégio Bandeirantes); Debora Schisler (Seven Idiomas); Helena Nagano (Cultura Inglesa); Alessandra de Campos (Alumni); Maria Lúcia Sciamarelli (Colégio Divina Providência); Catarina Kruppa (Cultura Inglesa); Roberto Costa (Freelance teacher/consultant); Patricia McKay Aronis (CEL-LEP); Claudia Beatriz Cavalieri (By the World Idiomas); Sérgio Lima (Vermont English School); Rita Miranda (IBI – [Instituto Batista de Idiomas]); Maria de Fátima Galery (Britain English School); Marlene Almeida (Teacher Trainer Consultant); Flávia Samarane (Colégio Logosófico); Maria Tereza Vianna (Greenwich Schools); Daniele Brauer (Cultura Inglesa/AMS Idiomas); Allessandra Cierno (Colégio Santa Dorotira); Helga Silva Nelken (Greenwich Schools/Colégio Edna Roriz); Regina Marta Bazzoni (Britain English School); Adriano Reis (Greenwich Schools); Vanessa Silva Freire de Andrade (Private teacher); Nilvane Guimarães (Colégio Santo Agostinho)

In Ecuador:

Santiago Proaño (Independent teacher trainer); Tania Abad (UDLA [Universidad de Las Americas]); Rosario Llerena (Colegio Isaac Newton); Paúl Viteri (Colegio Andino); Diego Maldonado (Central University); Verónica Vera (Colegio Tomás Moro); Mónica Sarauz (Colegio San Gabriel); Carolina Flores (Colegio APCH); Boris Cadena, Vinicio Reyes (Colegio Benalcázar); Deigo Ponce (Colegio Gonzaga); Byron Freire (Colegio Nuestra Señora del Rosario)

The authors and publisher would also like to thank the following contributors, script writers and collaborators for their inspired work in creating *Uncover*:
Anna Whitcher, Janet Gokay, Kathryn O'Dell, Lynne Robertson, Dana Henricks

Unit	Vocabulary	Grammar	Listening	Conversation (Useful language)
1 Life on the Edge pp. 2–11	■ Extreme weather ■ Basic needs	■ Simple present and present continuous review ■ Simple past and past continuous review ■ *used to* Grammar reference p. 106	■ Biking the Pan-American Highway	■ Agreeing and disagreeing
2 First Things First! pp. 12–21	■ Priorities ■ Emotions	■ *have to/don't have to* ■ *must* ■ Modals of obligation – *should, ought to, had better* ■ *It's* + adjective + infinitive Grammar reference p. 107	■ Take it easy!	■ Helping someone to do something
3 Art All Around Us pp. 22–31	■ Visual arts ■ Musical instruments	■ Verb + *-ing* form (gerund) review ■ *-ing* forms (gerunds) as subjects ■ Verbs + prepositions + *-ing* forms (gerunds) Grammar reference p. 108	■ Leo the one-man band	■ Inviting a friend and arranging to meet
4 Sign Me Up! pp. 32–41	■ Adventure travel ■ Phrasal verbs related to travel	■ Present perfect with *already, yet*, and *just* ■ Present perfect questions ■ Present perfect with *for* and *since* ■ *How long . . . ?* and the present perfect Grammar reference p. 109	■ Adventure travel experiences	■ Signing up for an adventure activity
5 Yikes! pp. 42–51	■ Fears ■ *-ed* and *-ing* adjective endings	■ Future review – *will, be going to*, present continuous ■ First conditional ■ Modals of probability – *must, can't, may, might, could* Grammar reference p. 110	■ Conversations at an amusement park	■ Expressing disbelief

Unit 1–5 Review Game pp. 52–53

Writing	Reading	Video	Accuracy and fluency	Speaking outcomes
A persuasive email	*Freezing in Siberia* Reading to write: *A fun vacation* Culture: *Tristan da Cunha*	*The Long Winter* *Which do you prefer, towns and cities or the country?* *An Island Flood* *The Khomani San of the Kalahari* (CLIL Project p. 116)	Not using *a* to talk about the weather Pronunciation of *used to*	I can . . . talk about extreme weather. discuss how my environment affects my life. talk about past incidents and habits. ask for agreement. discuss a faraway place.
A blog post about solving a problem	*Getting Some Shut-Eye* Reading to write: *Stories of Stress* Culture: *Ten Things I Bet You Didn't Know About . . . Cheerleading*	*Get Up and Go!* *What makes a good friend?* *Irish Dancing*	Using *to* after *ought*, *should*, and *had better* The letter *c*	I can . . . discuss my priorities. express obligation and prohibition. make strong recommendations. offer help to someone. discuss a sport or cultural activity.
A blog post about a concert	*Everyone's an Artist* Reading to write: *Fantastic Free Concert* Culture: *A Temporary Desert City*	*Original Art* *Have you ever been to a concert?* *A World of Music* *Art in Perspective* (CLIL Project p. 117)	Using the *-ing* form after *enjoy* Word stress with *love* and *hate* Spelling the *-ing* forms	I can . . . talk about visual arts. express my likes and dislikes. discuss music. make invitations and arrangements. discuss a cultural event.
An email comparing different customs	*Anchors Aweigh!* Reading to write: *Tipping help!* Culture: *Five Good Reasons to Visit New Zealand*	*The Age of Discovery* *What's the most exciting thing you've ever done?* *Fun in Australia*	Using *go* before activities that end in *-ing* Word stress with time words	I can . . . talk about adventure travel. ask and answer questions about personal experiences. ask and answer questions about the duration of activities. talk about signing up for an adventure activity. discuss reasons to visit a place.
An email to a friend about plans and problems	*Ask Maria* Reading to write: *Afraid to fly!* Culture: *Superstitions? Who needs them?!*	*Creepy Creatures* *What are you afraid of?* *Calendars of the Ancient Maya* *City vs. Country* (CLIL Project p. 118)	Pronunciation of *I'll* as /al/ Not using *must* for future probability	I can . . . identify and discuss common fears. talk about future events. talk about things that are possible and not possible. express disbelief. discuss superstitions.

1 Life on the Edge

Discovery EDUCATION

BE CURIOUS

The Long Winter

Which do you prefer – towns and cities or the country?

An Island Flood

Life in the Desert

1. What do you see in this picture?

2. Where do you think this kind of weather takes place? What other places have "extreme" weather?

3. What might be different about life in places with extreme weather?

UNIT CONTENTS

Vocabulary Extreme weather; basic needs
Grammar Simple present and present continuous review; simple past and past continuous review
Listening Biking the Pan-American Highway

Vocabulary: Extreme weather

1. Match the words and phrases with the correct pictures.

a b c d e f g

1. _g_ high winds
2. ___ blizzard
3. ___ hail
4. ___ heat wave
5. ___ thunder and lightning
6. ___ heavy rain
7. ___ fog

2. Listen, check, and repeat. (1.02)

3. Which of the words and phrases in Exercise 1 do you associate with a) very hot weather, b) very cold weather, c) hot or cold weather?

4. Think about where you live. When do you experience extreme weather? Write the words and phrases from Exercise 1 in the following categories.

> **Get it RIGHT!**
> Don't use the article *a* to talk about weather.
> Yakutsk has **very cold** weather.
> NOT: ~~Yakutsk has **a very cold** weather.~~

Sometimes in the summer	Sometimes in the winter	At least once a month	Only once or twice a year	Never

Speaking: What's it like outside?

5. **YOUR TURN** Work with a partner. Ask and answer the questions.
1. What other words do you know to describe weather?
2. What's the weather like today where you live?
3. What weather stories are in the news right now?

6. Talk to your partner about the weather where you live.

> We're having a bad heat wave this week. Right now it's 35°C!

▶ Workbook, p. 2

Reading Freezing in Siberia!; A fun vacation; Tristan da Cunha
Conversation Agreeing and disagreeing
Writing A persuasive email

The COLDEST TOWN on EARTH

Freezing in Siberia!

Yakutsk – the coldest town on Earth. From November to March, it's only light for three or four hours a day, and the temperature is hardly ever above freezing. The average daytime temperature is –30°C, and at night, it sometimes falls as low as –60°C. Now that's cold!

Right now, I'm writing on my computer in the library. It's warm inside, but outside, people are wearing heavy pants, tall boots, hats, scarves, and heavy coats. It often takes me half an hour to get ready to leave the house. When I get home, it takes me another half an hour to take off all those clothes!

Life in the extreme cold is difficult. At –20°C, the air freezes inside your nose. At –40°C, you can't stay outdoors for more than 10 minutes or your skin freezes. At –45°C, the metal on your glasses sticks to your face! I don't go out very much. People only walk short distances from one warm place to another. All activities happen indoors – from shopping to sports. A popular local sport that lots of boys do is wrestling. I don't wrestle. I like to jump rope, and I try to do it three or four times a week. Both jumping rope and wrestling use a lot of energy, and they keep you warm and strong. That's important when you live in subzero conditions!

In the summer, Yakutsk is a different city. In June and July, it's the season of "white nights," when the sky never gets dark, not even at midnight. The snow melts, and the temperature rises to 30°C and higher. Most people are happy to have a heat wave after 10 months of winter. Camping and barbecues are the favorite summer activities, with parties all night long. I'm thinking about summer weather a lot these days because there are still four more months of winter. I can't wait for summer!

DID YOU KNOW...?
The lowest ever recorded temperature in Yakutsk, Siberia, northeast Russia, was –64°C.

Reading: A blog

1. Look at the title of the blog. What is special about the town of Yakutsk?

2. Read and listen to Meg's blog. Check your answer in Exercise 1.

3. Read the blog again. Answer the questions.
   1. What are the average temperatures in Yakutsk in winter?
   2. What kinds of clothes do people wear outside in the winter?
   3. Why does it take a lot of time to get ready to go out in the winter?
   4. What is the season of "white nights"?
   5. What do people do in the summer in Yakutsk?

4. **YOUR TURN** Work with a partner. Ask and answer the questions.
   1. Would you like to live in Yakutsk? What are the good things about living there? What are the bad things?
   2. Are there any places in your country that are similar to Yakutsk?
   3. Which is the coldest region in your country? What's the hottest?
   4. How is life in your town different in summer and in winter? In what way?

   I wouldn't want to live in Yakutsk. It's too cold there!

Grammar: Simple present and present continuous review

5. Complete the chart.

Use the simple present to describe what normally happens. This includes routines and facts.	
The metal on your glasses **sticks** to your face.	I **don't like** hot weather.
I _____ cold weather. Winter **is** my favorite season.	We _____ **go out** a lot in the winter. It's too cold!
Use the present continuous to describe something happening right now or these days.	
I**'m wearing** a hat.	My friend **isn't studying** for tomorrow's test right now.
We**'re** _____ a lot of hot food like soup these days because it's cold outside.	I**'m not** _____ boots because it's too hot outside for them.

> Check your answers: Grammar reference, p. 106

6. Circle the correct answers.

1. **I'm trying** / **I try** to stay inside the house these days.
2. When the weather is bad, most activities **happen** / **are happening** indoors.
3. My friends **love** / **are loving** cold weather.
4. **We watch** / **We're watching** the weather report on TV right now.
5. In my town, the snow **melts** / **is melting** only in April or May.
6. Matthew **plans** / **is planning** his vacation in the Bahamas right now.
7. My cousin moved to Costa Rica because she **doesn't like** / **isn't liking** cold winters.
8. Right now, Daniel and Elizabeth **put** / **are putting** their boots on to walk to school.

7. Complete the text with the simple present or present continuous forms of the verbs. Listen and check.

Mark and his family ¹___*love*___ (love) the place they live: Costa Rica. But this week, they ²_____ (live) a different life. They ³_____ (visit) their cousins in Barrow, Alaska. Costa Rica is a warm, tropical country. The temperature ⁴_____ (not change) much there. It's around 27°C all year round. The average temperature in Barrow is 11°C, and the temperature ⁵_____ (stay) below 0°C for 160 days of the year. Mark's in Barrow right now. He says, "I ⁶_____ (have) fun with my cousins this week, but we ⁷_____ (not go) outside much. I ⁸_____ (not have) the right clothes!" In Costa Rica, Mark usually ⁹_____ (play) soccer outside after school, but this week, he ¹⁰_____ (play) video games indoors. In Costa Rica, he ¹¹_____ (go) to the beach on Saturday or Sunday. In Barrow, he ¹²_____ (go) to hockey games. He says, "I can't wait to get back to hot weather!"

Speaking: It's too hot!

8. YOUR TURN Make notes about how hot weather and cold weather affect you. Then ask and answer the questions with a partner.

- What do you eat?
- How well do you sleep?
- Where do you exercise?
- What do you do for fun?

> In really cold weather, I eat a lot of bread and soup. In really hot weather, I don't eat anything. I'm not hungry!

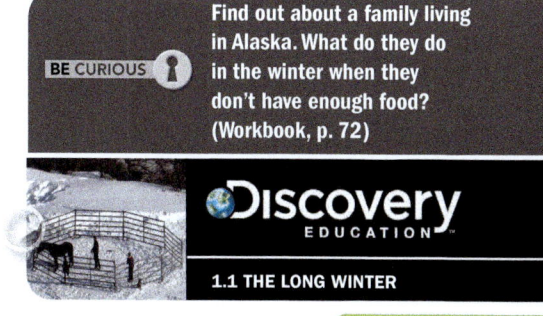

BE CURIOUS Find out about a family living in Alaska. What do they do in the winter when they don't have enough food? (Workbook, p. 72)

Discovery EDUCATION

1.1 THE LONG WINTER

On the ROAD

Listening: Biking the Pan-American Highway

1. Look at the map of the Pan-American Highway. How many kilometers do you imagine the highway is? How long do you think it would take to travel the entire highway by bike?

2. Listen to a radio program about a family's experience on the Pan-American Highway. How does Diane, the mother, feel now that the trip is finished?

3. Listen again. Circle the correct answers.

   1. How long is the Pan-American Highway?
      a. 28,000 kilometers   b. 100 kilometers   c. 13,000 kilometers

   2. In what country did the Miller family take a plane?
      a. Ecuador   b. Argentina   c. Panama

   3. How far did the family ride each day?
      a. between 11 and 13 kilometers
      b. between 14 and 16 kilometers
      c. between 50 and 100 kilometers

   4. How did the Miller family communicate with family members?
      a. They read blogs.
      b. They wrote a blog post every week.
      c. They talked on the phone.

   5. What did Robert miss the most while he was traveling?
      a. having a home   b. free entertainment
      c. going to a different place every night

   6. How can listeners find out more about the Millers' trip?
      a. They can send an email to Robert and Diane.
      b. They can read the blog or Diane's book.
      c. They can read Diane's book or call her on the phone.

Vocabulary: Basic needs

4. Match the words and phrases with the words associated with them. Then listen and check your answers.

   1. ___ food and drink   a. house, apartment
   2. ___ clothes   b. movies, games, sports
   3. ___ entertainment   c. high school, college, homeschooling
   4. ___ health care   d. email, text messages, phone calls
   5. ___ transportation   e. hospitals, laboratories, clinics
   6. ___ communication   f. spaghetti, salad, juice
   7. ___ a home   g. cash, credit cards, coins
   8. ___ education   h. buses, trucks, bikes
   9. ___ money   i. boots, jackets, hats

5. Look again at the words in Exercise 4. Write them in order of importance to you. Then discuss your list with your partner.

Grammar: Simple past and past continuous review

6. Complete the chart.

Use the simple past to describe actions and events in the past.	
We **took** a plane over part of Panama.	They **didn't have** to stop for food.
We _____ our own food.	He **didn't** _____ his arm, but it hurt a lot.
What _____ you **miss** the most?	
Use the past continuous to describe actions and events in progress in the past.	
I _____ **spending** the night in Quito when I heard that the road was closed.	He **wasn't wearing** a helmet when he fell.
They _____ **eating** their lunch by the road when the storm started.	You **weren't talking** to me when I dropped my phone.
What **were** you _____ last night when the electricity went out?	

> Check your answers: Grammar reference, p. 106

7. Circle the correct answers.

1. My bike **broke / was breaking** down while I **rode / was riding** through Mexico.
2. When she **studied / was studying** in Greece, Evelyn **bought / was buying** food from local markets.
3. I **sat / was sitting** in the park when I **heard / was hearing** the news.
4. When the hail **began / was beginning**, I **talked / was talking** on the phone.
5. You **called / were calling** while I **watched / was watching** the football game.
6. Neil and Austin **drove / were driving** through the blizzard when they **ran / were running** out of gas.

8. Complete the sentences with the correct form of *used to* and the verbs in parentheses.

1. I _____ (think) everyone in South America spoke Spanish, but now I know that people in Brazil speak Portuguese.
2. Steve _____ (not ride) his bike much, but now he rides it every day.
3. My grandparents _____ (not come) to see us often, but now they visit every month.
4. Public transportation _____ (be) terrible in this town, but now we have a great subway system.
5. We _____ (not cook) a lot of meals at home, but now we only go to restaurants on special occasions.

used to

Use *used to* when something happened over a period of time but doesn't happen anymore.

I **used to be** a swimmer, but now I play soccer.

We **didn't use to ride** our bikes a lot, but now we ride every day.

Did you **use to live** in Boston?

Speaking: Last night and long ago

9. YOUR TURN Use the phrases below to write five questions. You can use the simple past or past continuous.

what	do	last night
when	go	when you were younger
where	eat	
	live	

Say it RIGHT!

In statements, *used to* often sounds like /justə/. Listen and repeat the sentences.

I **used to** spend a lot of money on public transportation, but now I ride my bike.

He **used to** like living in Canada, but he doesn't anymore. It's too cold!

10. Work in pairs. Ask and answer your questions.

> What were you doing last night?

> I was doing my homework. What about you?

Workbook, pp. 4–5

REAL TALK 1.2 WHICH DO YOU PREFER – TOWNS AND CITIES OR THE COUNTRY?

A Great Place TO LIVE

Conversation: City, town, or country?

1. **REAL TALK** Watch or listen to the teenagers. Check (✓) the things that the teenagers like about living in the city.

   ☐ bike riding ☐ fresh air ☐ looking at animals
   ☐ concerts ☐ hiking ☐ different neighborhoods
   ☐ shopping ☐ museums ☐ parks

2. **YOUR TURN** Which do you prefer – small towns, cities, or the country? Tell your partner.

3. Listen to Kate talking to Mark about Greenville. Complete the conversation.

   USEFUL LANGUAGE: Agreeing and disagreeing

   don't you think? ✓Don't you agree? I don't think so. See what I mean? I disagree.

   Kate: Do you live near school, Mark?
   Mark: No, I live in Greenville. Have you been there?
   Kate: Yes, I live there, too. It's a great place to live. ¹ _Don't you agree?_
   Mark: Well, it's really quiet. Actually, nothing ever happens, and there's nothing to do. It's boring.
   Kate: Well, ² _____ There are lots of things to do. What about the new mall and the community center?
   Mark: Maybe, but all my friends live here, in the city, and I can't go out with them in the evening.
   Kate: Yeah, but Greenville is healthier, ³ _____
   Mark: The air, you mean? ⁴ _____ It's close to the city, so I don't think living in Greenville makes a difference. And there's so much heavy rain.
   Kate: Well, if there's heavy rain in Greenville, there's heavy rain in the city, too. They both have the same weather.
   Mark: That's true. I like taking my dog for walks. Greenville is good for that.
   Kate: ⁵ _____ It's not all bad.
   Mark: That's true. Maybe you're right. Small towns are OK, but I still wish I lived in the city.

4. Practice the conversation with a partner.

5. **YOUR TURN** Work with a partner. Take turns giving your opinion. Then agree and disagree.

Situation 1	Situation 2
Living in a city.	Going to a big school.
Good: lots to do, easy to travel around	Good: lots of facilities, clubs, variety of different subjects to study
Bad: noisy, stressful, unhealthy	Bad: noisy, impersonal, more bullying

   There's a lot to do in the city, and that's good, don't you think?

   Well, I like small towns. They're not as noisy as big cities. . . .

8 | Unit 1

To: laura@net.cup.org
From: addison@net.cup.org
Subject: A fun vacation

Hi Laura!

I'd like you to come visit me this summer. I miss you! You live in a big city, but I live in a cabin by a lake and that's cool, too. Ask your parents if you can spend a week with me and my family this summer. Here's what you can tell them:

First of all, we can do lots of fun stuff. For example, we can go swimming all day, every day. My family also has a boat, and we can go water skiing or visit other places on the lake. There's an island in the middle of the lake, and we can have a barbecue there.

Second, it's healthy to be out here by the lake. You'll get a lot of exercise. For instance, we can go hiking in the woods (and we can go swimming again when we come back!). We can shop for organic food at the farmers' market. And there's no pollution, and this part of the state is really clean and nice.

The best part is that we can be together! I haven't seen you in six months. That's a long time.

I really hope you can visit us this summer! Talk to your mom and dad. If they have any questions, they can talk to my parents.

Love,
Addison

Reading to write: A persuasive email

6. Look at the pictures and read Addison's email to Laura. What does she want Laura to do?

◉ Focus on CONTENT

When you write a persuasive email, you can follow this format:
- Start with a topic sentence that states your position on something.
- Explain why you think your readers should do what you're suggesting. Start your sentences with phrases such as *First of all*, *Second*, and *The best part*.
- Close your email by stating your position again. Try to say it in a different way this time.

7. Find examples of each of the points in Focus on Content in Addison's email.

◉ Focus on LANGUAGE

Introducing details
For example and *for instance* are similar in meaning.
- There's a lot to do in the city. **For Instance** / **For example**, you can visit art museums.

8. Match the sentences.

1. There are lots of fun things to do in the mountains. For example, ___
2. We have lots of different kinds of weather here. For instance, ___
3. There are lots of great restaurants in my town. For instance, ___
4. Mary eats an unhealthy amount of sugar every day. For example, ___

a. today she had doughnuts and soda for breakfast, an ice-cream sundae for dessert at lunch, and a big piece of cake at dinner.
b. we have Greek ones, Italian ones, and my favorite, a place that only serves pancakes.
c. you can ride horses, hike, or go camping.
d. we have blizzards in the winter, heavy rains in the spring, and heat waves in the summer.

Writing: A persuasive email

◻ PLAN
Think of something you'd like to persuade someone else to do. Use the list in the Focus on Content box and make notes.

◻ WRITE
Write your email. Use your notes from above to help you. Write about 150 words.

◻ CHECK
Check your writing. Can you say "yes" to these questions?
- Have you followed the instructions in the Focus on Content box?
- Did you use *for example* or *for instance*?

Tristan da Cunha

The most remote inhabited island on Earth!

Tristan da Cunha, the most remote inhabited island on the planet, is in the middle of the Atlantic Ocean. It's over 2,800 kilometers from the nearest land, and to get there, you need to fly to Cape Town, in South Africa. Then, because there's no airport on the island, you have to travel by ship for seven days.

Tristan da Cunha was named after the Portuguese discoverer who first saw the island. Although it is almost 10,000 kilometers from London, it's part of a British territory. The official language is English, but the people who live there also speak a local dialect. The British monarch is the head of state, and they use British pounds as their currency.

The island is very small – only 11 kilometers long. Queen Mary Peak, a volcano in the middle of the island, is 2,000 meters high, and it's active, too! The weather doesn't get too hot or too cold, but there are times of heavy rain.

The island is home to 80 families, about 260 people in total, and they have only eight last names. These are the last names of some of the first people to settle on the island. There is only one town and one school, and that's the only place with an Internet connection.

In October 1961, the island's volcano erupted, and the whole population went to live in the UK. They got jobs and new homes, but they didn't like living so far from their island. They weren't used to the noise, the traffic, and the cold winter. So, in November 1962, 200 islanders returned to Tristan da Cunha and their old lives there. They were happier without television, cars, and the stress of modern life!

DID YOU KNOW…?

Many of the original settlers of the island had asthma. Over 50 percent of the people on Tristan da Cunha have asthma now. Scientists have learned a lot about the disease by studying the people of the island.

Culture: A remote island

1. Look at the picture. Where do you think this place is? What is special about it?

2. Read and listen to the article. Check your answers in Exercise 1.

3. Read the article again. Complete the table.

Approximate distance from the nearest land:	2,800 kilometers
Official language:	
Approximate distance from London:	
Length of island:	
Number of families:	
Number of schools:	
Month and year that the volcano erupted:	
Number of people who returned to Tristan da Cunha in 1962:	

4. **YOUR TURN** Work with a partner. Ask and answer the questions.
   1. Would you like to visit Tristan da Cunha? Why? / Why not?
   2. What do you think are the good things about living on the island? What are the bad things?

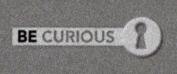

BE CURIOUS: Find out about the people in Bali, India. What are their two main foods? (Workbook, p. 73)

Discovery EDUCATION

1.3 AN ISLAND FLOOD

UNIT 1 REVIEW

Vocabulary

1. Write the extreme weather word for each picture.

1. _____fog_____ 2. _____

3. _____ 4. _____

5. _____ 6. _____

Grammar

2. Complete the sentences.

1. You can't go outside right now. It _'s raining_ (rain) really hard!
2. I _____ (work) after school and on the weekends to make extra money.
3. My teacher _____ (not talk) right now. She's writing a report at her desk.
4. We _____ (not like) cold weather. That's why we live in Florida.
5. My little brother _____ (cry) when there is thunder and lightning.
6. The chef is in the restaurant kitchen. He _____ (make) a special soup.

3. Circle the correct answers.

1. The surfer **swam / was swimming** in the ocean when she saw the shark.
2. When I was younger, I **watched / used to watch** a lot of TV. I don't anymore.
3. It **rained / used to rain** about 10 centimeters last night.
4. What **did you do / were you doing** at 9:00 p.m. last night?
5. My sister **wasn't thinking / didn't use to think** that education was important. Now she studies really hard.
6. I **did / was doing** all my homework. Do you want to play a video game?

Useful language

4. Complete the conversation.

| you agree | think |
| See what I | disagree |

John: Hey, Dylan. My family is taking a vacation abroad this summer. We might go to Canada.

Dylan: Canada? There are blizzards there! The weather is pretty harsh, don't you ¹_____?

John: Actually, it's nice in the summer. What about you? What are your plans?

Dylan: I want to learn Spanish. My friend Mike is visiting his grandma in Colombia, and he invited me to come. I can learn a lot of Spanish. Don't ²_____?

John: No. Mike's American. You won't learn Spanish.

Dylan: I ³_____. I can learn from his grandma!

John: Well, maybe you're right. It'll be fun, even if you don't learn a lot of Spanish.

Dylan: ⁴_____ mean? It's a great idea!

PROGRESS CHECK: Now I can . . .

- ☐ talk about extreme weather.
- ☐ discuss how my environment affects my life.
- ☐ talk about past incidents and habits.
- ☐ ask for agreement.
- ☐ write a persuasive email.
- ☐ discuss a faraway place.

CLIL PROJECT

1.4 LIFE IN THE DESERT, p. 116

Unit 1 | 11

2 First Things FIRST!

Discovery EDUCATION

BE CURIOUS

- Get Up and Go!
- What do you think makes a good friend?
- Irish Dancing

1. What do you see in this photo?

2. How busy are you? Do you have lots of different things going on in your life?

3. How do you feel about all your different activities?

UNIT CONTENTS

Vocabulary Priorities; emotions
Grammar have to/don't have to; must; Modals of obligation – should, ought to, had better; It's + adjective + infinitive
Listening Take it easy!

Vocabulary: Priorities

1. Match the photos (a–h) with the phrases.

1. _b_ shopping for clothes
2. ___ working out
3. ___ hanging out with friends
4. ___ doing something creative
5. ___ getting enough sleep
6. ___ having time for yourself
7. ___ helping around the house
8. ___ chatting with friends online
9. ___ staying out late on the weekend

2. Listen, check, and repeat.

3. What activities are the words below associated with? Write phrases from Exercise 1 in the correct place below.

1. making a cake or writing a song   _____
2. going to parties or movies at night   _____
3. lifting weights or doing exercises   _____
4. washing the dishes, cleaning your room   _____
5. taking a walk, reading a book   _____
6. watching TV, playing games, talking   _____

Speaking: What matters most?

4. YOUR TURN Work with a partner. Ask and answer the questions.

1. Which thing in the list in Exercise 1 is most important to you? Why?
2. Which things do you argue about with your parents?
3. Which thing stresses you the most? Why?

> Let's see. I think the most important thing for me is having time for myself – so I can just relax and do what I want to do!

Workbook, p. 8

Reading Getting Some Shut-Eye; Stories of Stress; Ten Things I Bet You Didn't Know About . . . Cheerleading
Conversation Helping someone to do something
Writing A blog post about solving a problem

Unit 2 | 13

Time for BED

Getting Some Shut-Eye

Did You Know?
Teenagers who sleep enough:
> usually have better skin than those who don't sleep enough.
> eat less junk food than teens who don't.
> are less likely to experience depression than those who don't.

Teenagers have to get more sleep! According to researchers, teenagers need to sleep a lot more than adults: eight to 10 hours every night. Sadly, only 15 percent of teenagers sleep eight hours on a school night, and that's just not enough.

Here are three reasons to get more sleep:

Your body needs sleep.
Your body is still growing, and your brain is still developing. Teenagers shouldn't forget how much their bodies need that extra sleep.

Sleep helps you do better in school.
When you're tired, you can't concentrate very well. And when you can't concentrate, it's difficult to learn.

Sleep keeps you healthy.
Without enough sleep, your body gets weak, and it's easy for you to catch colds and other illnesses. Tired people often eat food with more sugar in it, and that isn't good for you.

What can you do to get more sleep?
> Don't drink anything with caffeine at night, including soda.
> If you're hungry, have a light snack. That sometimes helps people sleep.
> One hour before you go to bed, turn off the TV and shut down your computer.
> Don't take your cell phone to bed with you!

Reading: A magazine article

1. Look at the picture. How many hours of sleep do you think teenagers need?

2. Read and listen to the article about teenagers and sleep. What's the main aim of the article?

   a. to tell parents what to do about teenagers who sleep a lot

   b. to offer advice to teenagers about how to get up earlier in the morning

   c. to tell teenagers why sleep is important and how to get more of it

3. Read the article again and answer the questions.

   1. What is one reason teenagers may feel depressed or sad?
   2. How many hours of sleep do most teenagers need?
   3. What percentage of teenagers sleep eight hours on school nights?
   4. What can happen at school if you don't get enough sleep?
   5. What kind of food do tired people usually eat more of?
   6. What should you do one hour before you go to bed?

4. **YOUR TURN** Work with a partner. Ask and answer the questions.

   1. What time do you usually go to bed during the week? Do you find it difficult to get to sleep? Why? / Why not?
   2. Do you think you get enough sleep? What kinds of things keep you from getting a good night's sleep? What happens if you don't sleep enough?

   What time do you usually go to bed during the week?

   I usually go to bed around 11:00. What about you?

Say it RIGHT!

Notice the different sounds of the letter *c*. Can you find another example of each in the article?

/s/ — ne**c**essary
/k/ — **c**affeine

Grammar: *have to/don't have to*

5. Complete the chart.

Use **have/has to** *to say that it is necessary to do something.*
Use **don't/doesn't have to** *to say that it is not necessary to do something, but you can do it if you want to.*

Affirmative	Negative
I _____ **get** more sleep.	I _____ **get up** early on Saturdays.
My brother _____ **get up** early on Saturdays. He works in a restaurant.	My little sister _____ **help** with the housework. She's only two.

> Check your answers: Grammar reference, p. 107

6. Complete the sentences with the correct form of *have to*.

1. A professional tennis player _____ train for four or five hours every day.

2. I _____ study math three or four hours every night. It's really difficult for me!

3. My mom is a piano teacher, so I _____ pay for my piano lessons.

4. My brother is really lucky. He _____ do any homework. He's only three years old.

5. My parents _____ work on weekends, so we usually do something fun together.

6. My best friend _____ get up early on Saturday. His baseball practice starts at 8:00 a.m.

7. Use the words to write sentences. Use *must* or *must not*.

must
Use **must/must not** *to talk about rules, laws, or prohibited actions.*

You **must** be quiet in the library.	You **must not** touch the art in a museum.
She **must** return her books on time.	He **must not** use his cell phone here.

1. You / eat in the classroom
   _____

2. You / wear your seat belt in the car
   _____

3. You / leave trash on the beach
   _____

4. You / come to school on time
   _____

5. You / clean up your trash when you go camping
   _____

6. You / take scissors on a plane
   _____

Speaking: *Do you have to . . . ?*

8. YOUR TURN Work with a partner. Ask and answer questions using *Do you have to . . .* and the phrases.

clean your room
get up early on Saturday or Sunday
go to bed at a specific time
help cook meals
practice a musical instrument
study English over the weekend
take care of your younger brother or sister
wash the dishes

> *Do you have to take care of your younger sister?*
>
> *Yes, sometimes I do, when my parents have to work late.*

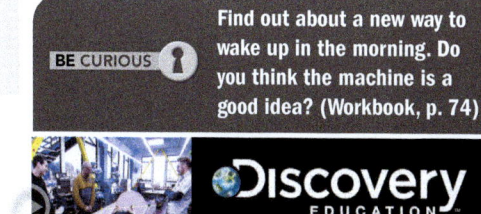

BE CURIOUS Find out about a new way to wake up in the morning. Do you think the machine is a good idea? (Workbook, p. 74)

Discovery EDUCATION
2.1 GET UP AND GO!

Stressed OUT!

Listening: Take it easy!

1. Look at the girl in the picture above. How does she feel? What are some reasons she might feel that way?

2. Listen to a radio interview with a psychologist, Dr. Hilary Jamieson, talking about teenage stress. What are the three essential tips Dr. Jamieson gives?

3. Listen again. Circle the things Dr. Jamieson suggests.
   1. Make a schedule and keep to it.
   2. Go out with your friends and have a good time.
   3. Participate in a sport.
   4. Listen to music or watch TV.
   5. Talk to someone.
   6. Breathe deeply and try to relax.

Vocabulary: Emotions

4. Match the words with the correct pictures. Then listen and check your answers.
   1. ___ embarrassed
   2. ___ awful
   3. ___ proud
   4. ___ terrified
   5. ___ stressed out
   6. ___ exhausted
   7. ___ wonderful

5. Think of a time when you or someone you know felt one of the emotions in Exercise 4. Tell your partner about it.

> I felt stressed out last week. I had a lot of homework, and my mother was mad at me, too.

> Really? I felt wonderful last week. This week I feel exhausted because . . .

Grammar: Modals of obligation – *should*, *ought to*, *had better*

6. Complete the chart.

Should, ought to, and had better have similar meanings. Use them to say what is a good or right thing to do.		
Use should and shouldn't for a personal opinion.	Use ought to and ought not to when you're talking about duty or the law.	Use had better and had better not to give very strong advice.
You **should try** to work out more.	I _____ **call** the police about the car accident.	You **had better start** studying for your test now.
He _____ **get** so stressed out.	You **ought not to enter** that part of the airport.	You _____ **be** late for the test.

> Check your answers: Grammar reference, p. 107

7. Choose the correct answers.

1. If you're sick, you **had better / had better not** see a doctor.
2. My brother doesn't know what he **should / shouldn't** do about college.
3. You **ought / ought not** to park your car here. It's illegal.
4. We **should / shouldn't** go see a movie when we have so much work to do.
5. She **ought / ought not** to be more careful when she's cooking. She always burns herself.
6. I **had better / had better not** bother my father right now. He's really busy.

8. Use the words in parentheses to write + (affirmative) or – (negative) sentences.

1. It's *not easy to find* enough time to study sometimes. (– / easy / to find)
2. It's _____ some exercise every day. (+ / important / to get)
3. It's _____ with friends on the weekend. (+ / relaxing / to hang out)
4. It's _____ too many after-school activities. (– / smart / to do)
5. It's _____ all your time studying. (– / fun / to spend)
6. It's _____ your arms and legs when you're taking a test. (+ / helpful / to stretch)

> **It's + adjective + infinitive**
> Use It's + adjective + infinitive to give your opinion.
> **It's important to talk** to others when you're stressed.
> **It's not helpful to think** negative thoughts.

> **Get it RIGHT!**
> Use *to* after *ought*.
> You **ought to call** the police.
>
> Don't use *to* after *should* or *had better*.
> You **should drink** less coffee.
> You **had better leave** for school now.

Speaking: Do I have to?

9. Read the situations below. Check (✓) the ones you have experienced.

- ☐ I'm really tired, but I have so much homework to do!
- ☐ I really want to get on the school team this year, but I need to practice hard!
- ☐ My parents got mad at me last night because I came home really late.
- ☐ I argued with my best friend, and now he/she won't respond to my texts.

10. YOUR TURN Work with a partner. Take turns reading each of the situations in Exercise 9 and giving advice.

> My parents got mad at me last night because I came home really late.

> You should call them next time and tell them where you are.

REAL TALK 2.2 WHAT DO YOU THINK MAKES A GOOD FRIEND?

Best Friends
FOREVER

Conversation: What makes a good friend?

1. **REAL TALK** Watch or listen to the teenagers. Check (✓) the things they say.

   ☐ buys good birthday presents
   ☐ does all the same activities
   ☐ just has to be there
   ☐ is kind and helpful
   ☐ helps with decisions
   ☐ helps with homework
   ☐ likes to go out on the weekend
   ☐ likes to talk on the phone
   ☐ listens
   ☐ is honest

2. What do you think makes a good friend? What would you add to the list above?

3. Listen to Olivia ask Laura about a school project. Complete the conversation.

   USEFUL LANGUAGE: Helping someone to do something

   I'm not very good at things like that.
   It's really pretty simple.
   ✓ I'm not sure how to do it.
   Let me show you.
   I'll give you a hand if you like.

   Olivia: Hey, Laura. Can I ask you something?
   Laura: Yeah, sure. What's up?
   Olivia: It's this science project. ¹_____*I'm not sure how to do it.*_____
   Laura: Mr. Brown's really strict about it. He put instructions on the school intranet.
   Olivia: Oh! I should look, then. Do you know how to get access to the intranet?
   Laura: Yes, you have to type in your password.
   ²_____ See? Type it like this, and click "Submit."
   Olivia: Thanks. That's really nice of you!
   Laura: ³_____ You shouldn't have any problems with it. Just make sure you format it correctly.
   Olivia: Oh, no! ⁴_____
   Laura: Don't worry. ⁵_____
   Olivia: Great! Thanks a lot.

4. Practice the conversation with a partner.

5. **YOUR TURN** Work with a partner. Take turns asking for and giving help. Use the following ideas or your own ideas.

   Situation 1: You want to download a video, but you don't know how.
   Possible steps: Find the video; click on the "Download" button; name the video and click "Save."

   Situation 2: You can't find any material for a school project.
   Possible steps: Find online sources; go to the library; find people to interview.

Stories of STRESS

STUDYING HARD?
STRESSED OUT?
TOO MUCH TO DO?

Tell us your story. What was the problem and how did you feel? How did you solve it and what's your advice to students with similar problems? We publish the best stories on our website!

MIKE, SAN DIEGO, CA: I have a story to tell about a time last month when I had too much to do. And I think I have some great advice. The problem was that I had a big history test and besides that, I had a lot of other projects to do, too. I was super stressed out. I was studying hard one Saturday afternoon, for about three hours straight. Then a friend came over. He helped me solve the problem. He said, "Take a little time off!" We had a snack, and then we took my dog for a walk. Then I started studying again. What happened? I was relaxed, I had more energy, and I was able to study for the rest of the day. Best of all, I got an A on the test! My advice: You have to take a break sometimes.

Reading to write: Solving a problem

◉ *Focus on* **CONTENT**
When you're writing about a solution to a problem, it's necessary to tell the reader what the problem is. Then tell the reader your solution to the problem in clear steps. You can write these steps in order of their importance. Start with the most important step.

6. Read Mike's blog post. Answer the questions.

1. What was the problem?
2. How did Mike feel?
3. How did he solve it?
4. What is Mike's advice to other students?

◉ *Focus on* **LANGUAGE**
Quantifiers: *a few, a little, too many, too much*
- Use *a few* and *a little* to talk about a small amount or number. Use *a few* with plural countable nouns, and *a little* with uncountable nouns.
  - *We played a video game for* **a few** *minutes.*
  - *I decided to take* **a little** *time off.*
- Use *too many* and *too much* to talk about things that are "more than is good for the situation."
  - *I had* **too many** *other projects to do.*
  - *He said I was studying* **too much**.

Writing: A blog post

▢ **PLAN**
Think about a time you were stressed out or had too much to do. What was the problem? How did you feel and how did you solve it? What's your advice to other students who have the same problem?

▢ **WRITE**
Write your blog post. Use your notes from Exercise 6 and Mike's story to help you. Write 80–100 words.

▢ **CHECK**
Check your writing. Can you answer "yes" to these questions?
- Did you say what the problem is?
- Did you give a solution in clear steps?
- Did you state the steps to the solution in order of importance?

7. Complete the sentences with *a few*, *a little*, *too many*, and *too much*.

1. David only has _____ books in his backpack. It isn't heavy.
2. I brought _____ food for lunch today. Would you like half of this sandwich?
3. There were _____ people in line for the movie, so we left without seeing it.
4. I can go to bed early because I only have _____ homework today.

Ten Things I Bet You Didn't Know About...
CHEERLEADING

1 Cheerleading is more than 100 years old! The first cheerleading team came out to support the University of Minnesota football team in November 1889.

2 Today, more than 97 percent of all cheerleaders are female, but 100 years ago they were all male.

3 Now, on college or university cheerleading squads in the United States, half of the members are male.

4 Cheerleading is very competitive, and it's difficult to make most squads. The successful candidates often have to spend their summers training together for the next season.

5 Football is the main sport associated with cheerleading, but there are also cheerleaders for basketball, soccer, baseball, and even wrestling!

6 Cheerleading is a great way to fight stress. It also helps you feel good and make friends!

7 Cheerleading won't hurt your grades! It's important to have discipline – as an athlete and as a student. Cheerleading helps with this.

8 Cheerleading is hard physical work. Cheerleaders train hard – as hard as the football players they support – and they have to be very fit. Ninety-eight percent of female cheerleaders are also gymnasts.

9 Cheerleading can be dangerous. Many cheerleaders injure their arms and legs. Some also injure their backs and heads.

10 Cheerleading started in the United States and is still very much an American activity, but there are organized cheerleaders in more than 31 countries around the world.

Culture: Cheerleading

1. **Look at the photos and answer the questions.**
   1. Where are the people? What are they doing?
   2. What do you know about cheerleading? Make a list.

2. **Read and listen to the article. Does it mention any of the facts you wrote in Exercise 1?**

3. **Read the article again. Are the sentences below true (*T*) or false (*F*)?**
   1. All cheerleaders are girls. ___
   2. Cheerleaders only support football teams. ___
   3. Most cheerleaders don't do well in school. ___
   4. Cheerleading is hard work. ___
   5. Cheerleading is a very safe activity. ___
   6. Cheerleaders only exist in the United States. ___

4. **YOUR TURN Work with a partner. Ask and answer the questions.**
   1. Would you like to be a cheerleader? Why? / Why not?
   2. Why do you think cheerleading helps students' grades?
   3. What are the most popular school sports and activities in your country? Do you think these sports can help you do better in school? Why? / Why not?

DID YOU KNOW...?
There are more than 4 million cheerleaders in the world.

BE CURIOUS Find out about an Irish dance champion. How is Irish dance different from dance in your country? (Workbook, p. 75)

Discovery EDUCATION
2.3 IRISH DANCING

UNIT 2 REVIEW

Vocabulary

1. Complete the sentences.

| get enough sleep | do something creative |
| time for myself | help around the house |

1. I need to be alone sometimes. I need _____.
2. My mom sometimes asks me to _____. I hate cleaning the bathroom!
3. I'm always tired because I don't _____.
4. I want to be a designer or an artist because I want to _____.

2. Match the sentences.

1. I just fell down in the hall outside of class. ___
2. I just ran five kilometers! ___
3. I have four big tests this week. ___
4. My sister's volleyball team just won a big game. ___

a. I'm proud of them.
b. I'm really stressed out.
c. I'm exhausted.
d. I'm so embarrassed!

Grammar

3. Write sentences with should (✓) or shouldn't (✗).

1. You / play computer games in the evening (✗)
   You shouldn't play computer games in the evening.
2. Teenagers / help their families on the weekends (✓)
   _____
3. You / use your cell phone before bed (✗)
   _____
4. My sister is stressed out. She / talk to a friend (✓)
   _____
5. Teenagers / eat healthy food whenever they can (✓)
   _____
6. I / watch TV right now (✗)
   _____

4. Fill in the blanks with the correct form of *have to*.

1. You ____have to____ be quiet in the library.
2. The basketball game is free. We _____ pay for tickets.
3. Julio wears jeans and T-shirts to school. He _____ wear a uniform.
4. Students _____ eat in the cafeteria. They are allowed to leave the school for lunch.
5. Mike _____ study for his math test tonight. He can't go out.

Useful language

5. Complete the conversation.

| Let me show you. | I'm not very good at things like that. | I'm not sure how to do it. |

Kate: Oh, no.
Pete: Are you OK? What do you need?
Kate: I'm just stressed out about my science homework. ¹_____ I need some coffee, I think.
Pete: Don't drink coffee now. Make some herbal tea.
Kate: Make herbal tea? ²_____
Pete: Look. ³_____ It's easy.
Kate: It is?
Pete: Yes. Boil some water and pour it over a tea bag. Like this.
Kate: That *was* easy. Hey, this tea is good!

PROGRESS CHECK: Now I can . . .

☐ discuss my priorities.
☐ express obligation and prohibition.
☐ write a blog post to help someone solve a problem.
☐ make strong recommendations.
☐ offer help to someone.
☐ discuss a sport or cultural activity.

UNITS 1–2 REVIEW, Workbook, pp. 14–15

3 ART All Around Us

Discovery EDUCATION
BE CURIOUS

- Original Art
- Have you ever been to a concert?
- A World of Music
- Art in Perspective

1. Describe what you see in this picture.

2. What is your opinion of this kind of art?

3. In what ways is this kind of art different from art you see in museums?

UNIT CONTENTS

Vocabulary Visual arts; musical instruments
Grammar Verb + -ing form (gerund) review; -ing forms (gerunds) as subjects; verbs + prepositions + -ing forms
Listening Leo the one-man band

Vocabulary: Visual arts

1. Match the people, places, and things with the correct pictures.

   1. _g_ comics
   2. ___ living statue
   3. ___ digital art
   4. ___ sculpture
   5. ___ drawing
   6. ___ mural
   7. ___ exhibition
   8. ___ pottery
   9. ___ graffiti
   10. ___ portrait painter

2. Listen, check, and repeat.

3. Put the words from Exercise 1 in the correct categories.

   a. Works of art: _____

   b. Place to see art: _____

   c. A performer or an artist: _____

Speaking: Look again

4. **YOUR TURN** Put the words from Exercise 1 in new categories.

Cool	Educational	Strange

5. Work with a partner. Share your opinions about kinds of art.

   I like looking at comics. They're really cool.

▶ Workbook, p. 16

Reading Everyone's an Artist; Fantastic Free Concert; A Temporary Desert City
Conversation Inviting a friend and arranging to meet
Writing A blog post about a concert

WHAT is ART?

EVERYONE'S AN ARTIST

You draw, you paint portraits, you do sculptures, or you're a living statue. It doesn't matter — everyone's an artist!

THE CASE FOR We look at the *Mona Lisa* or a Picasso painting, and we say, "That's art." But what about the amazing graffiti on your street? What about photographs posted online by our friends? What about your school art exhibition? You worked hard, and it's great. So, is that art? To me, art is anything that's creative. Of course, I like going to famous museums. But I also like drawing portraits of my friends. I'm not very good, but I'm creative. I'm passionate about it, and my friends like it. Most of all, I like it!

Josh, age 15, San Diego, California

THE CASE AGAINST I like visiting art museums, too. Why? Because I like looking at good art. Art is not the drawings of four-year-old children. It isn't painting your body crazy colors and standing in the street. And it certainly isn't graffiti. Some people say, "If it's creative and cool, it's art." I don't agree. Art is the result of hard work and study. My aunt is an artist. She went to art school for six years. She doesn't make much money, but sometimes her sculptures are in exhibitions. Her art is great. Art is very hard, and not many people can do it well.

Kayla, age 16, Charlotte, North Carolina

WHAT IS ART? WHAT'S YOUR OPINION?

DID YOU KNOW...?
The British graffiti artist Banksy sold a piece of graffiti for $1.8 million.

Reading: An online debate

1. **Work with a partner. Ask and answer the questions.**
    1. Do you ever see art that you think is terrible? Why do you think it's bad?
    2. What makes a person an artist?
    3. Do you have friends or family members who are artists?

2. **Read and listen to the debate. How do Josh and Kayla define "art"?**

3. **Read the debate again. Are the statements true (T) or false (F)?**
    1. Josh thinks that graffiti is art. ___
    2. Kayla enjoys going to art museums. ___
    3. To Josh, photographs posted online aren't examples of art. ___
    4. Kayla believes that art is anything that is creative and fun. ___
    5. Josh and his friends like the portraits he draws. ___
    6. Kayla thinks that good art is easy. ___

4. **YOUR TURN Work with a partner. Ask and answer the questions.**
    1. What's your opinion in the art debate? Is everyone an artist?
    2. What kind of background or education do you think an artist should have?
    3. Is graffiti art? If so, is all graffiti art or only some graffiti?
    4. Are pictures you take with your cell phone and then post online art? Why or why not?

> I think graffiti is sometimes good art. There's an artist in my neighborhood who . . .

Grammar: Verb + -ing form (gerund) review

5. Complete the chart.

We can use the -ing form of a verb after some verbs to talk about things we like or don't like.

Common verbs followed by -ing forms:
like, love, hate, enjoy, (not) mind

	-ing form		
I **love**	_drawing_	(draw)	pictures in my free time.
Mark **enjoys**	_____	(look)	at sculptures.
My sister **hates**	_____	(help)	around the house.
Some people **don't like**	_____	(go)	to museums.

> Check your answers: Grammar reference, p. 108

Get it RIGHT!
Use the -ing form after *enjoy*.
I **enjoy going** to art exhibitions. NOT:
I ~~enjoy to go~~ to art exhibitions.

Say it RIGHT!
When you like or don't like something strongly, use *love* or *hate* and put extra stress on that verb. Listen and repeat the sentences.
I **love** painting. I **hate** shopping.

6. Complete the sentences with the correct forms of the verbs.

1. My friends ____love going____ (love / go) to the movies on the weekends.
2. I _____ (not mind / spend) time at art exhibits, but not more than two hours at a time.
3. Oscar _____ (enjoy / paint) murals, but not portraits.
4. My father _____ (not like / shop) for clothes. He never goes to the mall.
5. Some of my friends _____ (hate / read) comics, but I enjoy it a lot.
6. I _____ (like / study) in the library, not alone at home.

7. Circle the correct answers. Then complete the sentences.

| get up | ✓ live | paint | take |
| go | meet | sleep | work out |

My name is Jill, and I'm a professional artist. I live in Los Angeles. I ¹**like / don't like** ___living___ here because Los Angeles is full of open-minded, creative people. Mornings are my favorite time of the day, and I ²**love / hate** _____ early. Because it's sunny but not hot outside, I really ³**hate / like** _____ a long walk before I start work. It's great exercise. I usually paint for a few hours, maybe from 9:00 to 12:00, and then I have lunch. I ⁴**don't enjoy / enjoy** _____ friends for lunch. We usually make lunch together. After lunch, I ⁵**like / don't mind** _____ for about 30 minutes. Then I go back to work. I ⁶**finish / keep** _____ in the evening, about 7:00 or 8:00 p.m. I ⁷**love / don't love** _____ at the gym or going running on the beach. And, I ⁸**like / hate** _____ to bed late. I'm usually asleep by 9:00 or 10:00. It's a busy life, but I'm happy.

Speaking: I love shopping!

8. YOUR TURN Work with a partner. Tell your partner about the things you like and don't like doing.

Like	Don't like
don't mind, enjoy, like, love	don't enjoy, don't like, hate

> *I like staying up late at night. I don't enjoy getting up early!*

BE CURIOUS Find out about Aboriginal paintings in Australia. Do they represent the land, water, or air? (Workbook, p. 76)

Discovery EDUCATION

3.1 ORIGINAL ART

MUSIC Everywhere!

Listening: Leo the one-man band

1. What do you imagine a one-man band is? Where do you think he performs?

2. 🔊 3.04 Listen to Marcia, a journalist, interviewing Leo. Check your answers in Exercise 1.

3. 🔊 3.04 Listen again. Answer the questions.
   1. Where are Marcia and Leo?
   2. Where are two places that Leo plays music?
   3. Which of Leo's instruments is new?
   4. How long did Leo play on the day of the interview?
   5. What types of music does he like playing?
   6. Which instruments does he not know how to play?

Vocabulary: Musical instruments

4. 🔊 3.05 Match the words with the correct pictures. Then listen and check your answers.

   1. ___ guitar
   2. ___ drums
   3. ___ flute
   4. ___ saxophone
   5. ___ violin
   6. ___ keyboard
   7. ___ harmonica
   8. ___ piano
   9. ___ trumpet
   10. ___ cello

5. **YOUR TURN** Work with a partner. Ask and answer the questions.
   1. What instruments can you play? How long did it take to learn to play them?
   2. What kind of music do you enjoy listening to?
   3. Where can you go in your town to listen to musicians playing in the street?

26 | Unit 3

Grammar: -ing forms (gerunds) as subjects

6. Complete the chart.

> You can use the -ing form as the subject of a sentence.
> ___Playing___ (play) several instruments at once takes a lot of energy.
> _____ (sing) at the same time I play instruments is hard.
> _____ (be) here at the festival is really special to me.
>
> For the negative, use not before the -ing form.
>
> **Not enjoying** some kinds of music is normal. You don't have to like everything.

▶ Check your answers: Grammar reference, p. 108

7. Match the phrases to make sentences.

1. Learning ___
2. Running ___
3. Singing ___
4. Reading ___
5. Drinking ___
6. Eating ___

a. in a heavy metal band can be hard on your voice.
b. lots of books is a good way to improve your writing skills.
c. a new instrument takes a lot of practice.
d. a lot of fresh fruit and vegetables is good for you.
e. in a marathon requires a lot of athletic ability.
f. soda every day is bad for your teeth.

8. Rewrite the sentences.

1. It's difficult to play three instruments at the same time.
   Playing three instruments at the same time is difficult.

2. It's important to practice for at least an hour a day.
   _____

3. It's not a good idea to take a test on an empty stomach.
   _____

4. It's exciting to have your art in an exhibit.
   _____

5. It isn't cheap to take private music lessons every week.
   _____

6. It's fun to be able to play an instrument well.
   _____

> ➤ **Spell it RIGHT!**
>
> **Spelling the -ing forms:**
> fix – fix**ing**   work – work**ing**
> If the verb ends in a silent -e, remove the -e and add -ing.
> live – liv**ing**   dance – danc**ing**
> If a verb ends in a vowel + a consonant, double the consonant.
> hug – hug**ging**   run – run**ning**

Speaking: Are you open-minded about music?

9. YOUR TURN Do you agree or disagree with the statements below?

1. I enjoy listening to all kinds of music.
2. Calling some kinds of music "bad" isn't right. If people like it, it's good music for them.
3. Listening to my friends' music is fun, even if it's not my style.
4. I like discovering new bands or singers.

> **Verbs + prepositions + -ing forms (gerunds)**
>
> You can use the -ing form after some verbs and prepositions.
>
> I want to **apologize for missing** your art exhibition.
>
> Do you **feel like going** to a movie tonight?
>
> This year, Allison needs to **concentrate on studying**, not **hanging out** with her friends.

10. Discuss your answers to Exercise 9 with a partner. Do you agree on everything? Then tell another pair about your partner's answers.

> Kim likes finding new bands, but she doesn't like all kinds of music. Her sister listens to pop music, and Kim hates that!

▶ Workbook, pp. 18–19

REAL TALK 3.2 HAVE YOU EVER BEEN TO A CONCERT?

Ready to ROCK?

Conversation: Have you ever been to a concert?

1. **REAL TALK** Watch or listen to the teenagers. Check (✓) the sentences you hear.

   ☐ I've played in some.
   ☐ I prefer going to the cinema (movies).
   ☐ Concert tickets are cheaper than movie tickets.
   ☐ I've been to seven or eight concerts.
   ☐ I love listening to music with a lot of people around.
   ☐ Live music is the best!

2. **YOUR TURN** Have you ever been to a concert? Who did you see? What were the good things and the bad things about the concert?

3. Listen to Mia and Austin talking about a concert. Complete the conversation.

> **USEFUL LANGUAGE: Inviting a friend and arranging to meet**
>
> ✓ How about going . . . ?   That's a good idea.   Should I ask . . . to take us?
>
> Sounds good.   What time should we meet?

Mia: Hey Austin! ¹ _How about going_ to a concert tomorrow?
Austin: Yeah, why not? Who's playing?
Mia: A pop rock band called The Sweets. They're a new band. I got free tickets.
Austin: Sure. ² _____ Where are they playing?
Mia: The Apollo Club, on Washington Street.
Austin: OK. ³ _____
Mia: It starts at 8:30. I think we should go together. How about meeting at my house at 7:30?
Austin: OK. ⁴ _____
Mia: Yeah! ⁵ _____ Then maybe my mom could pick us up when it's finished.
Austin: OK. See you tomorrow, then.

4. Practice the conversation with a partner.

5. **YOUR TURN** Work with a partner. Take turns inviting your friend and arranging to meet. Use the ideas below or your own ideas. Use the conversation in Exercise 3 as a model.

> **Concert 1**
> The Roots Boyz (reggae)
> The Hacienda Club
> 1315 Second Avenue
> Doors open: 8:00 p.m.
>
> **Concert 2**
> Live concert with Don't Be Shy (pop rock)
> The Black Bee Soul Club
> 2580 Lake Street
> Doors open: 8:30 p.m.

FANTASTIC FREE CONCERT

I just came back from a fantastic free concert. It was in a park about three kilometers from my house, and there was a great atmosphere. There were hundreds of young people there, dancing and enjoying themselves. There were about five bands, but the best one was Hurricane. They're from Cleveland, Ohio, and they play a mixture of lots of different styles, from folk and rock to reggae and blues. I loved listening to the singer (Layla Smith). She has a really amazing voice, and the guitarists and drummer played together really well. They just recorded a CD, and I want to get it! Seeing them play live was great. If you get the chance to see them, go for it! ☺

–Alba

Reading to write: A blog post about a concert

6. Look at the picture and read Alba's blog about a concert. Did she enjoy it?

> ### Focus on CONTENT
> **When you write about a concert, you can include this information:**
> - Where it was
> - The audience
> - Who played
> - The styles of music
> - Information about the band(s)
> - Why you liked or didn't like the music

7. Read Alba's blog again. Make notes on the items in the Focus on Content box.

> ### Focus on LANGUAGE
> **Singular and plural forms of *be***
> There **was** a great atmosphere. The best band **was** Hurricane. They (the band members) **are** from Cleveland, Ohio.

8. Find more examples of singular and plural forms of *be* in the blog post.

9. Complete the sentences with the present or past form of the verb *be*.

1. In my opinion, they ___are___ the best rock band on the planet!
2. There _____ a lot of people at the concert last night, from age 15 to 50.
3. Most of the people here at the concert tonight _____ obviously big fans of the group, singing every song!
4. The audience at last night's show _____ tiny, so there _____ (not) a very good atmosphere.
5. The band _____ (not) famous right now, but I think they will be soon.
6. All the musicians _____ very professional, but the music _____ (not) usually very exciting.

Writing: A blog post about a concert

☐ PLAN
Plan a blog post about a concert you've been to. Use the list in the Focus on Content box and make notes.

☐ WRITE
Write your blog post. Use your notes from Exercise 7 to help you. Write about 120 words.

☐ CHECK
Can you say "yes" to these questions?

- Is the information from the Focus on Content box in your writing?
- Did you get all the verbs in the correct singular or plural forms?

A Temporary DESERT CITY

So, some friends have just given you tickets to the Burning Man festival, but you're not sure what to expect. Read these frequently asked questions to find out more:

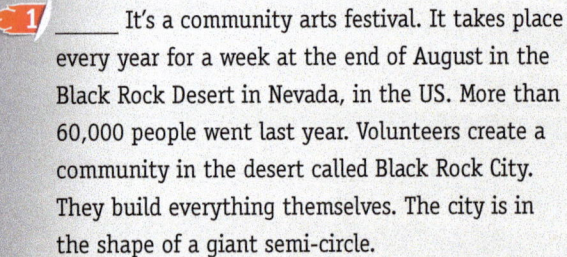

1 _____ It's a community arts festival. It takes place every year for a week at the end of August in the Black Rock Desert in Nevada, in the US. More than 60,000 people went last year. Volunteers create a community in the desert called Black Rock City. They build everything themselves. The city is in the shape of a giant semi-circle.

2 _____ No, it started in San Francisco, California, in 1986, next to the Golden Gate Bridge. It moved to the desert five years later.

3 _____ Because fire is an important theme of the festival. People build an enormous wooden statue of a person, more than 30 meters tall, and burn it during the festival. They also build and burn lots of other things. Last year, they had an enormous mechanical octopus!

4 _____ They dress up in crazy costumes. They also wear goggles and masks, which protect them from breathing the desert's dust. Besides that, there are a lot of other fun activities. There is usually a balloon chain of 450 different balloons. The chain is one kilometer long and it lights up the sky.

5 _____ When the festival ends, people must take everything away with them and leave the desert exactly as it was before the festival started. The organizers worry about damaging the environment.

6 _____ It's unusual because there aren't any famous bands or celebrities. Hanging out together as a community is what it's all about – everyone is on the same level.

Culture: The Burning Man festival

1. Look at the picture of a festival in the US. What do you think people do there?

2. Read and listen to the article. Check your answer in Exercise 1.

3. Read the article again. Match the questions (a–f) to the answers (1–6) in the article.
   a. What else do people do at the festival?
   b. Has the festival always taken place there?
   c. What happens after the festival?
   d. What is the Burning Man festival?
   e. How is it different from other festivals?
   f. Why is it called the Burning Man festival?

4. **YOUR TURN** Work with a partner. Ask and answer the questions.
   1. Would you like to go to a festival like Burning Man? Why? / Why not?
   2. Does your school or town have its own festival? What type of festival is it? What can you do there?

DID YOU KNOW…?
Every August, Black Rock City becomes the third largest city in Nevada – but then it disappears in September!

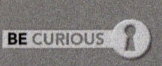

BE CURIOUS Find out about three different kinds of music. What three countries do the kinds of music come from? (Workbook, p. 77)

Discovery EDUCATION
3.3 A WORLD OF MUSIC

UNIT 3 REVIEW

Vocabulary

1. **Complete the sentences.**

   | comics | exhibition | living statue |
   | ✓ graffiti | sculptures | mural |

   1. There's some new ____graffiti____ on the wall outside the library.
   2. I love _____ that are made of stone or metal.
   3. There's an amazing _____ in the cafeteria at school. It covers one long wall.
   4. My brother is a big fan of superhero _____. He buys a lot of them.
   5. I went to an _____ of modern paintings last weekend.
   6. One of my friends makes a little money on weekends as a _____. He paints his body silver and wears all silver clothes.

Grammar

2. **Write sentences with the simple present and the -ing form of the verb.**

   1. my aunt / like / play / the guitar
      ____My aunt likes playing the guitar.____
   2. Mark and David / hate / sing / in music class
      _____
   3. the president of the company / not mind / walk / to work
      _____
   4. I / love / practice / the piano
      _____
   5. the artist / enjoy / paint / by the river
      _____
   6. the festival's participants / not like / sit / in the rain
      _____

3. **Complete the sentences.**

   1. My friends and I talk about ____making____ a music video, but we never do it. (make)
   2. _____ a lot is important if you want to become a good musician. (practice)
   3. _____ in big festivals is fun, but not everyone likes it. (participate)
   4. Did you decide against _____ to play the saxophone? (learn)
   5. In my opinion, _____ graffiti on walls is a terrible thing to do. (paint)
   6. My father isn't thinking about _____ abroad this year. (travel)

Useful language

4. **Complete the conversation.**

   | What time | ✓ going | Should I | good idea | Sure |

   Kyle: Hey Jenna. How about ¹____going____ to a street festival with me?
   Jenna: A street festival? Where?
   Kyle: Downtown. There will be lots of people playing music on the street for free. There's going to be lots of food there, too. I really want to go.
   Jenna: ²_____. Sounds great! ³_____ should we meet?
   Kyle: It's from 12:00 p.m. to midnight. How about going for lunch, around 1:00?
   Jenna: That's good. ⁴_____ ask my mom to take us?
   Kyle: That's a ⁵_____ ! She doesn't mind taking us, does she?
   Jenna: No, I don't think so. She might want to see the festival, too.
   Kyle: Perfect. See you at 1:00, then?
   Jenna: Yes. See you then!

PROGRESS CHECK: Now I can . . .
- ☐ talk about visual arts.
- ☐ express my likes and dislikes.
- ☐ discuss music.
- ☐ make invitations and arrangements.
- ☐ write about a concert that I've been to.
- ☐ discuss a cultural event.

CLIL PROJECT
3.4 ART IN PERSPECTIVE, p. 117

4 Sign Me UP!

Discovery EDUCATION

BE CURIOUS

The Age of Discovery

What's the most exciting thing you've ever done?

Fun in Australia

1. Describe what you see in this picture.
2. How does this picture make you feel?
3. Do you think this kind of sport would be fun?

UNIT CONTENTS

Vocabulary Adventure travel; phrasal verbs related to travel
Grammar Present perfect with *already*, *yet*, *just*, and *yes/no* questions; present perfect with *for*, *since*, and *How long . . . ?*
Listening Adventure travel experiences

Vocabulary: Adventure travel

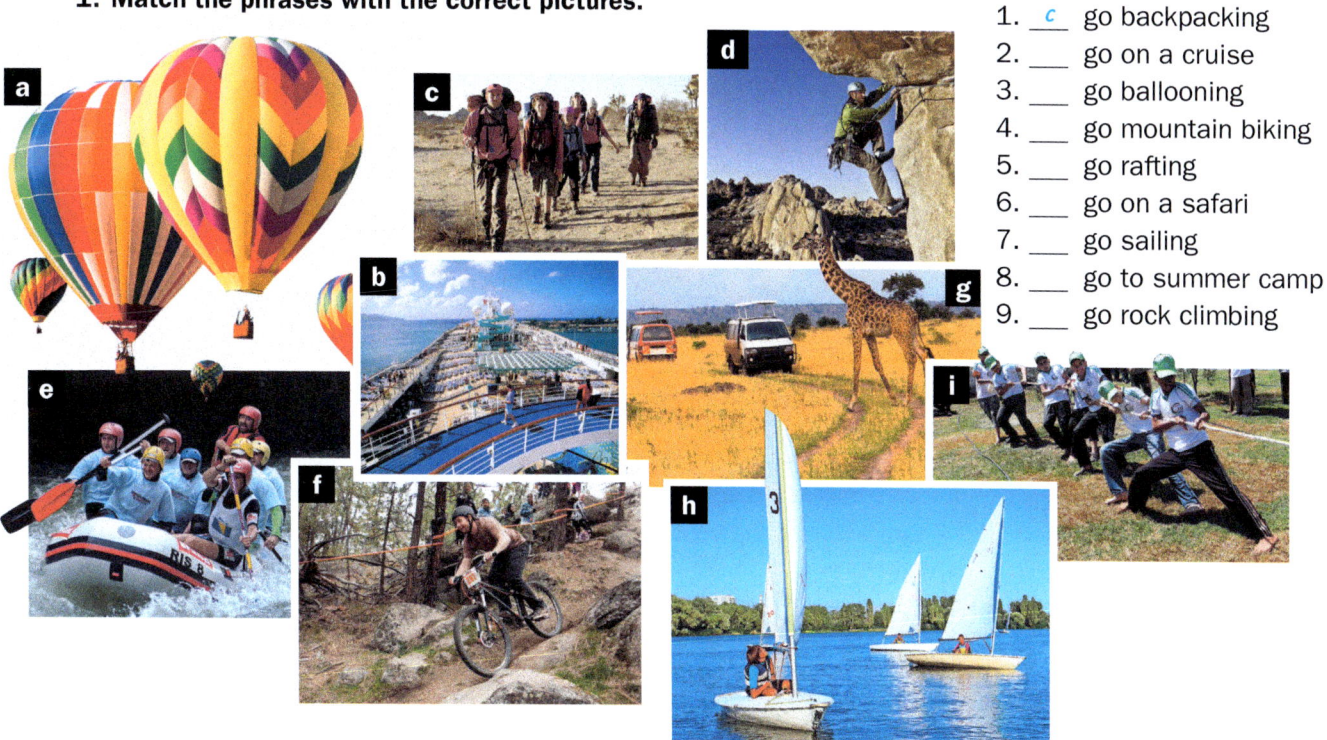

1. Match the phrases with the correct pictures.

   1. _c_ go backpacking
   2. ___ go on a cruise
   3. ___ go ballooning
   4. ___ go mountain biking
   5. ___ go rafting
   6. ___ go on a safari
   7. ___ go sailing
   8. ___ go to summer camp
   9. ___ go rock climbing

2. Listen, check, and repeat.

3. Which of the activities in Exercise 1 involve:
   a. participating in a sport?
   b. sleeping away from home?
   c. using some kind of transportation?

Get it RIGHT!

We use *go* before activities that end in *-ing*.
You can **go rafting** near here. NOT:
You can do rafting around here.

Speaking: I'm in!

4. **YOUR TURN** Work in groups of three or four. Ask and answer the questions and write the results.

   How many students . . .
   a. would like to go rafting?
   b. have gone to a summer camp?
   c. would definitely not want to go rock climbing?
   d. have been on a cruise?
   e. are afraid of going ballooning?
   f. have sailed in a small sailboat?

5. Tell your results to the class. Make a class chart.

   Twelve people in the class would enjoy going on a cruise.

   Twelve? I have fifteen. Fifteen people would enjoy going on a cruise.

▶ Workbook, p. 22

Reading Anchors Aweigh!; Tipping help!; Five Good Reasons to Visit New Zealand
Conversation Signing up for an adventure activity
Writing An email comparing different customs

Take to
THE WAVES

ANCHORS AWEIGH!

"I've never sailed before. This is my first time, and it's an amazing feeling." Sandra, 16, is on the *Stavros S. Niarchos*, a 70-meter sailing ship, with 40 other young sailors. The *Stavros* is an exact copy of the ships that pirates sailed two or three hundred years ago. It belongs to the Tall Ships Youth Trust. The Trust offers sailing trips at realistic prices for teenagers and young adults. Every year, thousands of young people get their first taste of the sea thanks to the Trust. Up to 70 percent of them are disabled or disadvantaged. For everyone, it's a once-in-a-lifetime experience.

Sandra is on a trip from the Azores, in the North Atlantic, to Spain. The trip lasts a week, and they have already been at sea for three days. "We do everything," she explained. "We sail the ship, we cook, we clean, and we take turns keeping watch at night. I never knew there was so much work on a ship!"

Her friend, Emma, 15, has never been on a boat before either. "I haven't adjusted to life at sea yet. It's very different from life on land!"

"We've done some cool stuff," says James, 17. "My favorite part is climbing the mast. It's 30 meters tall! The views are incredible," said James. "We've just seen dolphins and turtles for the first time. We haven't seen any whales yet, but the captain says there are whales near the Spanish coast. This is definitely the best thing I've ever done!"

If you want to know more about the Tall Ships Youth Trust, visit their website at tallships.org.

Reading: An online article

1. **Look at the title and the pictures. What kind of trip is it? Are the teenagers working, having fun, or both?**

2. **Read and listen to the article. Check your answers in Exercise 1.**

3. **Read the article again. What does each of the numbers refer to?**

   1. 70: ____length of the ship in meters____; _____

   2. 40: _____

   3. two or three hundred: _____

   4. thousands: _____

   5. 15: _____

   6. 30: _____

4. **YOUR TURN** Work with a partner. Ask and answer the questions.

   1. What do you think you can learn on a sailing trip like this?

   2. What are two reasons you would enjoy sailing on a boat like this? What are two reasons you wouldn't enjoy it?

   > *I think you can learn about yourself on a trip like this.*

   > *What do you mean?*

DID YOU KNOW...?
Over 95,000 people have sailed 1.8 million nautical miles with the Tall Ships Youth Trust.

Grammar: Present perfect with *already*, *yet*, and *just*

5. Complete the chart.

We can use *already* in affirmative sentences in the present perfect.	
I've **already been** at sea for four days.	He _____ _____ **cooked** three meals for the others on the ship.
We can use *yet* in negative sentences in the present perfect.	
They **haven't found** turtles **yet**.	My sister _____ **visited** the ship _____.
Use *just* with the present perfect to say that something happened very recently.	
We've **just seen** dolphins.	I _____ _____ **boarded** the ship.

Check your answers: Grammar reference, p. 109

6. Look at the chart. Complete the sentences with *already*, *yet*, or *just*.

1. I'm sorry, but the ship has ___already___ left. It left about three hours ago.
2. We haven't sailed alone _____.
3. I've _____ seen a whale! Look! Over there!
4. The boat hasn't left the port _____.
5. She's _____ been on three trips this year.
6. I've _____ finished lunch. It was delicious.

Present perfect questions

We can use *yet* in present perfect questions to ask if something has happened before now.

Have you seen any whales **yet**?	Yes, I have. / No, I haven't.
Has the ship arrived in Spain **yet**?	Yes, it has. / No, it hasn't.

7. Complete the conversation with the present perfect. Then listen and check.

A: Are you ready for the trip?

B: Well, sort of. ¹ _I haven't packed everything yet_ (I / not pack / everything / yet), but I know what I want to take.

A: Did you print your tickets?

B: No, not yet. ² _____ (Sam / not send / them / yet).

A: ³ _____ (you / do / anything / yet)?

B: Yes! ⁴ _____ (I / already / pack / my clothes).

A: What about your cell phone?

B: ⁵ _____ (I / just / put / my charger / in my bag), but I'm not going to take my tablet. There's no Internet connection on the ship.

A: And your passport?

B: Yes, don't worry, Mom! ⁶ _____ (I / already / check / that). It's in my purse.

Speaking: New experiences

8. YOUR TURN Work with a partner. Look at the activities, and interview each other. Ask your partner five questions using *already*, *yet*, and *just* about what he or she has done so far this year.

burn any food	send a text message to the wrong person
climb in a window	stay up all night
hurt yourself or break a bone	take a hike
lose your keys	wear socks that don't match

Have you lost your keys yet this year?

Yes, I have. / No, I haven't.

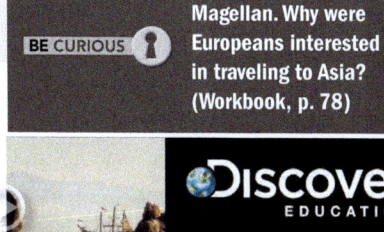

BE CURIOUS Find out about Ferdinand Magellan. Why were Europeans interested in traveling to Asia? (Workbook, p. 78)

Discovery EDUCATION

4.1 THE AGE OF DISCOVERY

Workbook, p. 23

Fun? It was INCREDIBLE!

Listening: Adventure travel experiences

1. **Look at the pictures of teenagers on vacation in Rocky Mountain National Park, in Colorado. Do their activities look like fun to you?**

2. **Listen to three short conversations with some of the teenagers in the pictures. Which sentence best summarizes how they feel about the trip?**
   a. They all love everything about their trips.
   b. They think Rocky Mountain National Park is really boring.
   c. They like some of the things they're doing more than other things.

3. **Listen again. Answer the questions.**
   1. How long has Lily been at the national park? What has she just finished doing?
   2. Does Evan love backpacking? Where did he go yesterday afternoon?
   3. How long has Katie been a rock climber? Which of Katie's family members is with her?

Vocabulary: Phrasal verbs related to travel

4. **Complete the sentences with the correct phrasal verbs. Then listen and check your answers.**

✓ come back	look around	make sure
find out	look forward to	take off
give up	look out	

   1. I really, really want to _____*come back*_____ here!
   2. _____ – that wall is going to fall down any minute!
   3. You played a good game, and I can't possibly beat you. I _____.
   4. Fasten your seat belts. The plane is about to _____.
   5. I _____ going on vacation this year.
   6. I like to _____ about new trails.
   7. You need to _____ to check your equipment.
   8. Let's have lunch up there and _____ a little.

5. **YOUR TURN Work with a partner. Ask and answer the questions.**
   1. What is something you look forward to doing in the next year?
   2. What are two things you make sure to do before you go to school every day?
   3. After tourists visit your city, what is something that they want to come back and do again?
   4. Before you visit a new place, do you like to find out all about it first?
   5. When you feel tired or you want to give up, what do you do?
   6. When you go to the mall with your friends, do you know exactly what you want, or do you prefer to just go and look around for a while?

   I look forward to going rafting. It sounds super fun!

Grammar: Present perfect with *for* and *since*

6. Complete the chart.

Use the present perfect with *for* or *since* for past actions and events continuing into the present.	
Use *for* with a period of time such as a week, two months, or five years.	
I've been here **for** three days.	He _____ **worked** at the rafting company _____ a month.
Use *since* with a specific date or time.	
They _____ **been** here _____ last Wednesday.	She**'s lived** in Colorado **since** 2010.

> Check your answers: Grammar reference, p. 109

7. Complete the sentences with *for* or *since*.

1. She's led safari tours every month _____ last November.
2. We've been backpacking in the park _____ Friday.
3. He hasn't gone on a cruise _____ three years, but he loves them.
4. We've played football together _____ 2011.
5. I've lived in Colorado _____ four years.
6. They've looked forward to this vacation _____ a long time.

8. Complete the conversation with the correct words.

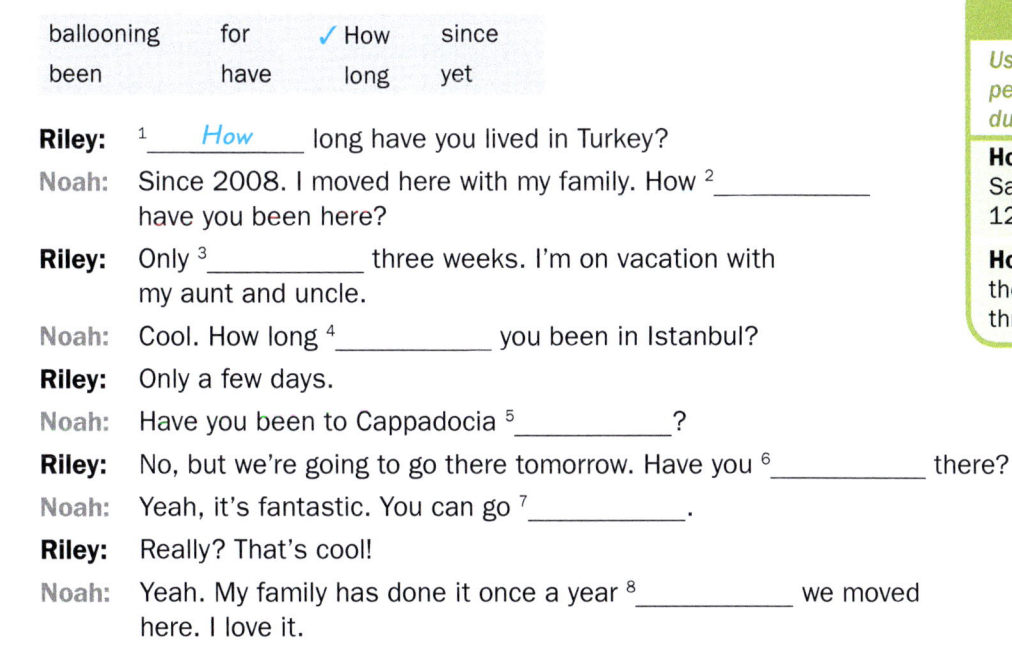

ballooning	for	✓ How	since
been	have	long	yet

Riley: ¹___How___ long have you lived in Turkey?
Noah: Since 2008. I moved here with my family. How ²_____ have you been here?
Riley: Only ³_____ three weeks. I'm on vacation with my aunt and uncle.
Noah: Cool. How long ⁴_____ you been in Istanbul?
Riley: Only a few days.
Noah: Have you been to Cappadocia ⁵_____?
Riley: No, but we're going to go there tomorrow. Have you ⁶_____ there?
Noah: Yeah, it's fantastic. You can go ⁷_____.
Riley: Really? That's cool!
Noah: Yeah. My family has done it once a year ⁸_____ we moved here. I love it.

How long . . . ? and the present perfect

Use *How long* and the present perfect to ask about the duration of an action or event.

How long have you lived in San Diego? (since 2008 / for 12 years)

How long has she been on the ship? (since July / for three months)

Speaking: I can't wait to do it again!

9. YOUR TURN Work with a partner. Choose three activities, and ask if your partner has ever done them. Then ask additional questions to continue the conversation.

fly in an airplane	go rock climbing	go to summer camp	travel to Africa
go ballooning	go sailing	travel by ship	travel to the US

> Have you ever traveled to the US?
>> Yes, I have.
> How long were you there?

Say it RIGHT!

When you answer questions with *How long . . . ?*, say the time words with more emphasis than the rest of the sentence. Listen and repeat the question and answer.
How long have you lived in Buenos Aires?
I've lived here for **three years**.

REAL TALK — 4.2 WHAT'S THE MOST EXCITING THING YOU'VE EVER DONE?

No experience NEEDED!

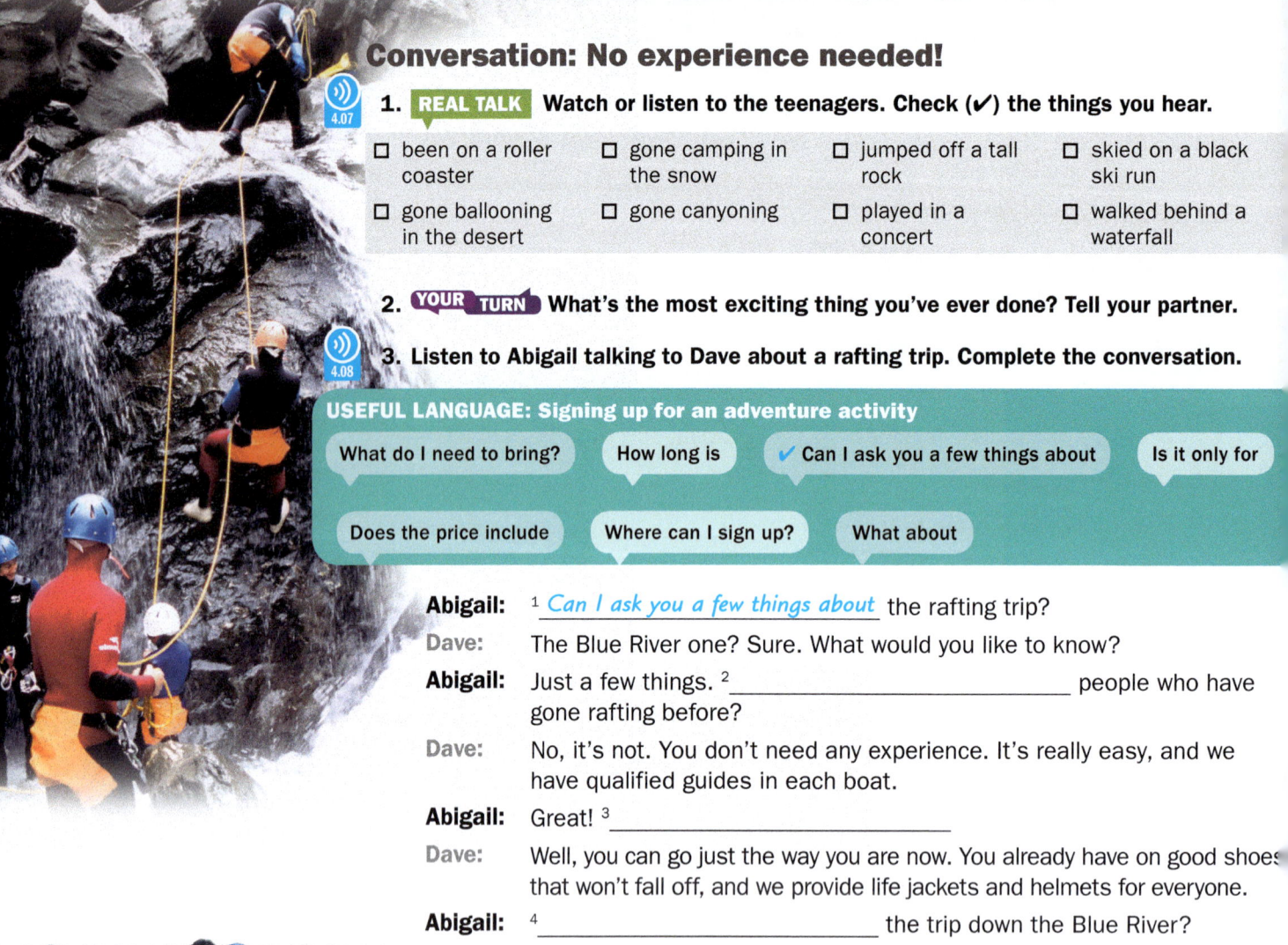

Conversation: No experience needed!

1. **REAL TALK** Watch or listen to the teenagers. Check (✓) the things you hear.

   ☐ been on a roller coaster
   ☐ gone camping in the snow
   ☐ jumped off a tall rock
   ☐ skied on a black ski run
   ☐ gone ballooning in the desert
   ☐ gone canyoning
   ☐ played in a concert
   ☐ walked behind a waterfall

2. **YOUR TURN** What's the most exciting thing you've ever done? Tell your partner.

3. Listen to Abigail talking to Dave about a rafting trip. Complete the conversation.

   USEFUL LANGUAGE: Signing up for an adventure activity

   What do I need to bring?   How long is   ✓ Can I ask you a few things about   Is it only for

   Does the price include   Where can I sign up?   What about

   Abigail: ¹ *Can I ask you a few things about* the rafting trip?
   Dave: The Blue River one? Sure. What would you like to know?
   Abigail: Just a few things. ² _____ people who have gone rafting before?
   Dave: No, it's not. You don't need any experience. It's really easy, and we have qualified guides in each boat.
   Abigail: Great! ³ _____
   Dave: Well, you can go just the way you are now. You already have on good shoes that won't fall off, and we provide life jackets and helmets for everyone.
   Abigail: ⁴ _____ the trip down the Blue River?
   Dave: It's all day, from 9:00 to 6:00.
   Abigail: OK. ⁵ _____ food?
   Dave: Food is included in the price.
   Abigail: ⁶ _____ transportation?
   Dave: Yes. We take you to the river and drop you off back here when the trip is finished. We handle everything, so you can just enjoy the adventure.
   Abigail: It sounds really fun. ⁷ _____
   Dave: Right here!

4. Practice the conversation with a partner.

5. **YOUR TURN** Work with a partner. Take turns asking about the activities below.

Activity 1	Activity 2
Sailing in the ocean with qualified instructors.	Rock climbing on Red Mountain with qualified instructors
We provide: life jacket, hot drinks on Belle Island	We provide: rock-climbing equipment, helmets, transportation to Red Mountain
You bring: swimsuit and towel, warm clothes	You bring: appropriate clothing for weather, good tennis shoes or rock-climbing shoes
Transportation from hotel to beach not included.	All day 10:00 to 5:00
Morning (9:00–12:00) or afternoon (3:00–6:00)	

To: audrey@net.cup.org
From: jean-claude@net.cup.org
Subject: Tipping help!

Dear Audrey,

How are you doing? I wonder if you could help me with something. I was recently on a mountain biking trip in Europe with some Americans. When we ate in restaurants, I did what we do in France: I either left a small tip, or I didn't leave a tip at all. Not only did the Americans leave a big tip (sometimes 20 percent or more of the bill!), but they also thought I was rude because I didn't. I can't believe Americans give the waiter that much money each time they eat out. Next month, I'm going to visit these friends in California for a biking trip there. You're American, but you've lived in France. What is the correct thing to do when we eat out?

Sincerely,
Jean-Claude

Dear Jean-Claude,

Wow! I'm not surprised you're confused. Although people tip waiters in both France and in the United States, tipping practices are different. In France, the tip – a service fee – is included in the bill. When I've been in France, I've sometimes left a few coins, or I've left as much as a euro for a meal. In the United States, however, waiters make very small salaries, and service is not included in the bill. Waiters depend on tips to survive, so Americans always leave a tip. Be prepared to add 15 to 20 percent to everything you order in a restaurant in the United States. And have fun biking!

Sincerely,
Audrey

Reading to write: An email comparing different customs

6. Look at the picture. Do you know what the money we leave a server in a restaurant is called? Read the emails and find out.

> ### ◉ Focus on CONTENT
> **Comparing**
> When you're comparing two different customs, be sure to compare the same topic for both places. Choose one topic at a time and compare how each place deals with the topic.

7. Look at the emails again. Answer the questions.

1. What topic is Jean-Claude writing about?
2. What is the custom in France?
3. What is the custom in the United States?

> ### ◉ Focus on LANGUAGE
> **Conjunctions**
> Use conjunctions to show relationships between ideas.
> both . . . and
> either . . . or
> not only . . . but also
> however
> although

8. Find one example of each conjunction in the emails.

Workbook, pp. 26–27

✏️ Writing: An email comparing different customs

▢ PLAN
Think of something from your country that might be confusing to someone from a different country. This could be greeting people, hand gestures, things people do (or don't do) in public, the things people do to have fun, or unique foods.

▢ WRITE
Write an email to an imaginary friend from another country. Use the email above to help you. Write about 120 words.

▢ CHECK
Can you say "yes" to these questions?

- Is the information from the Focus on Content box in your writing? Are you comparing the same thing in both cultures?

- Did you use conjunctions to show relationships between ideas?

Five Good Reasons to Visit NEW ZEALAND

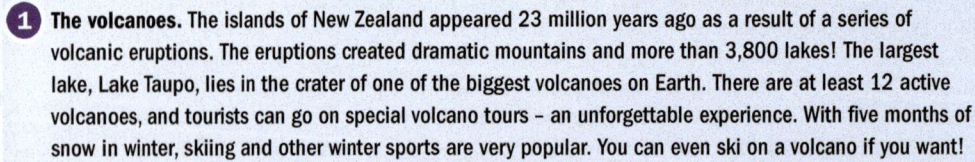

a

b

c

d

e

1. **The volcanoes.** The islands of New Zealand appeared 23 million years ago as a result of a series of volcanic eruptions. The eruptions created dramatic mountains and more than 3,800 lakes! The largest lake, Lake Taupo, lies in the crater of one of the biggest volcanoes on Earth. There are at least 12 active volcanoes, and tourists can go on special volcano tours – an unforgettable experience. With five months of snow in winter, skiing and other winter sports are very popular. You can even ski on a volcano if you want!

2. **The forests.** More than 30 percent of New Zealand is forest. Some of the forests have remained unchanged for millions of years. They're old, beautiful, and mysterious! They have made New Zealand a perfect choice for film directors. Did you know that the forests, lakes, and mountains were the settings for several important Hollywood movies like *The Hobbit*, *The Lord of the Rings*, and *The Chronicles of Narnia*?

3. **The beaches.** New Zealand has more than 6,000 kilometers of coastline. The beaches are long and sandy, and the conditions are perfect for water sports. Kayaking, diving, surfing, and sailing are all popular sports with locals and visitors. You can't visit New Zealand without visiting at least one of its fantastic beaches!

4. **The whales and dolphins.** Half of the world's whale and dolphin population lives in the seas around New Zealand. Kaikoura, on the South Island, is one of the best whale-watching spots in the world. If you've never seen a whale up close, this is your chance, and you shouldn't miss it.

5. **The culture.** Humans have only lived on the islands for about 1,000 years. The first people to arrive were islanders from Eastern Polynesia, called Maori. Today, about 15 percent of the population of New Zealand is Maori. Their culture and their customs developed into the Maori way of life. Maori language, literature, music, dance, sports, and even TV are all important in New Zealand. If you're in New Zealand, you should visit a *marae* – a Maori community facility – or even learn to speak the language.

Culture: New Zealand

1. **Look at the pictures of different outdoor activities that you can see or do in New Zealand. Answer the questions.**
   1. Have you ever done any of the activities?
   2. Which of the activities would you like to try?

2. **Read and listen to the article. Match the photos from Exercise 1 to the reasons for visiting New Zealand.**
   1. ____ 2. ____ 3. ____ 4. ____ 5. ____

3. **Read the article again. Find the numbers in the box in the article and explain what they refer to.**

23 million years ago	30 percent	1,000 years
3,800	millions of years	15 percent
12	6,000 kilometers	
five months	half	

4. **YOUR TURN** Work with a partner. Ask and answer the questions.
   1. Would you like to go to New Zealand? Why? / Why not?
   2. What outdoor activities can you do in and around your town or city?
   3. Do you have a favorite outdoor activity? If so, what is it? Why do you like it?

DID YOU KNOW...?
The human population of New Zealand is four million. The sheep population is 36 million!

BE CURIOUS Find out about some of the things that make Australia unusual. What unusual sport happens in Alice Springs? (Workbook, p. 79)

Discovery EDUCATION

4.3 FUN IN AUSTRALIA

UNIT 4 REVIEW

Vocabulary

1. **Complete the sentences with the activities.**

go backpacking	go on a cruise	go sailing
go ballooning	go on a safari	✓ go to summer camp

1. If you _go to summer camp,_ you'll make friends and learn new skills with kids your own age.
2. Let's _____! My father bought a new boat and he wants to go out on the lake.
3. We're going to _____ while we're in South Africa. I hope we see lions.
4. I'd love to _____. It must be fun to be on a big ship with swimming pools!
5. My brother wants to _____ for four days. I don't understand why because he hates walking. He won't even walk our dog!
6. I'm going to _____ in New Mexico again next week. I love floating along in the air, quietly looking down at the ground.

Grammar

2. **Seth and Mary are planning a weekend trip to the mountains. Write sentences or questions using the present perfect.**

1. Seth and Mary / buy a guidebook / already
   Seth and Mary have already bought a guidebook.
2. Mary / not reserve a place to camp / yet
   _____
3. Seth / pack his backpack / yet ?
   _____
4. Mary / check the weather report / just
   _____
5. They / not fill the car with gas / yet
   _____

3. **Write *for* or *since* to complete the phrases.**

1. _for_ a long time
2. _____ a year
3. _____ January 10
4. _____ Monday
5. _____ 10 days
6. _____ two weeks

Useful language

4. **Complete the conversation.**

about transportation	do I	include	Where
✓ Can I		how	Is it only

Nick: Hi! ¹ _Can I_ ask you a few things about the mountain biking trip?
Gabriella: Yeah. What would you like to know?
Nick: I've done a lot of biking, but I haven't gone mountain biking yet. ² _____ for people who have already done it?
Gabriella: No, this is on beginner trails. It's easy.
Nick: OK. What ³_____ need to bring?
Gabriella: Nothing. Just wear tennis shoes and comfortable clothes. We supply the helmets and the bikes.
Nick: Cool. What ⁴_____ to the start of the trail? Do you drive us there?
Gabriella: No, but there's a parking lot right there. You can drive and park your car there and meet us. Or you can walk. It isn't far at all.
Nick: OK. And ⁵_____ long is the trip?
Gabriella: All day, from 9:00 a.m. to 4:00 p.m.
Nick: Does the price ⁶_____ lunch?
Gabriella: Yes, and two snacks.
Nick: Cool! ⁷_____ can I sign up?

PROGRESS CHECK: Now I can . . .

☐ talk about adventure travel.
☐ ask and answer questions about personal experiences.
☐ ask and answer questions about the duration of activities.
☐ talk about signing up for an adventure activity.
☐ write about different customs.
☐ discuss reasons to visit a place.

5 Yikes!

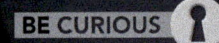

Discovery EDUCATION
BE CURIOUS

- Creepy Creatures
- What are you afraid of? 
- Calendars of the Ancient Maya 
- City or Country? 

1. Describe what you see in this picture.
2. How does this picture make you feel?
3. What kinds of things make you feel afraid?

UNIT CONTENTS
Vocabulary Fears; -ed and -ing adjective endings
Grammar Future review; first conditional; modals of probability – must, can't, may, might, could
Listening Conversations at an amusement park

Vocabulary: Fears

1. Match the photos (a–h) with the words.

1. __e__ flying
2. ____ heights
3. ____ the dark
4. ____ elevators
5. ____ insects
6. ____ birds
7. ____ clowns
8. ____ snakes

2. Listen, check, and repeat.

3. Match the comments about fears to the words in Exercise 1.

1. "I'm worried they might fly in through an open window and scratch me, or they might get into my hair!" _____
2. "I can't look out the windows of tall buildings. I get dizzy and have to sit down!" _____
3. "They're supposed to be funny, but their faces are really scary!" _____
4. "I always take the stairs." _____
5. "I sleep with a light on every night." _____
6. "I prefer to travel by train or car than by plane." _____
7. "I hate it when one flies into my face! I don't care how small it is, I always jump." _____
8. "I'm terrified when I'm out in the woods. I carry a stick and watch the grass for them." _____

Speaking: Reactions to fear

4. YOUR TURN Talk to three people in your class. Answer the questions below.

1. Do you know anyone who has any of these fears or other common ones?
2. How does the fear change his or her behavior?

Person	Fear	Behavior changes
Anna	flying	drives long distances to avoid planes

5. Tell your partner about the people you know and their fears.

> *My mother has a fear of flying. She drives really long distances to avoid going on a plane!*

> Workbook, p. 30

Reading Ask Maria; Afraid to fly!; Superstitions? Who Needs Them?!
Conversation Expressing disbelief

HELP!

Ask MARIA

Today we're going to look at fears and phobias. Everybody's afraid of something – elevators, insects, snakes – and famous people have fears, too. Did you know that Daniel Radcliffe is scared of clowns, Orlando Bloom is scared of pigs, and Nicole Kidman is scared of butterflies? For Justin Timberlake, it's spiders, and for Matt Damon, snakes. For most people, these fears aren't very important. However, when a fear becomes a phobia – an extreme and uncontrollable fear – it can cause serious problems.

Carlos, 14 (California)

"I can't sleep at night without a light, and sometimes it can be embarrassing. Next week, I'm traveling to New York on a school trip, and I'm going to share a room with other students. I don't want them to think I'm a baby! Please help. I'm really worried!"

Don't be embarrassed. Did you know that Keanu Reeves is afraid of the dark? And no one says he's a baby! Don't worry about what other people will think of you. Just tell your roommates that you want the light on at night like it's the most normal thing in the world.

Isabella, 13 (Florida)

"My uncle is getting married next month, and my mom, my dad, and I are going to the wedding – in Las Vegas! The problem is that I'm terrified of flying, and the flight to Las Vegas takes four and a half hours. What am I going to do?"

Lots of people are afraid of flying. Jennifer Aniston, for example, hates planes, so you're in good company! Try to relax before the flight. If you get some exercise, you'll feel tired, and then maybe you can sleep. Listen to your favorite music. When you feel nervous, close your eyes, and take long, deep breaths. If you do just one or two of these things, you'll be fine!

Reading: An advice column

1. Look at the famous people in the pictures. What do you think they're afraid of?

2. Read and listen to the online advice column and check your answers to the question in Exercise 1.

3. Read the advice column again and answer the questions.
   1. What is the difference between a fear and a phobia?
   2. Why does Isabella have to travel?
   3. What is Maria's advice to Isabella?
   4. Why does Carlos have to travel?
   5. What is Carlos worried about?
   6. What is Maria's advice to Carlos?

4. **YOUR TURN** Work with a partner. Ask and answer the questions.
   1. Do you think Maria gave good advice?
   2. Do you know of any other famous people who have fears or phobias? What are their fears?
   3. Do you think it's easy to help people with phobias? Why or why not?

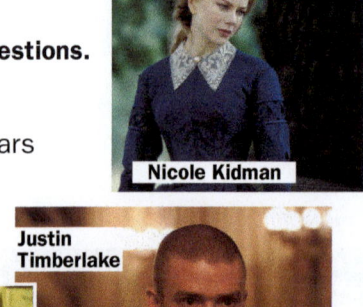

DID YOU KNOW...?

Arachnophobia – fear of spiders – is the most common phobia. Fifty percent of all women suffer from arachnophobia.

Grammar: Future review – *will*, *be going to*, present continuous

5. Complete the chart.

> Use *will, be going to,* and the present continuous to talk about the future.
> Use *will* for actions and events that we decide to do in the moment of speaking.
> Are you going running now? I _____ (go) with you.
> Use *going to* for planned actions and events. They may be in the near future or in a more distant future time.
> My brother and his friends are _____ (be) in different schools next year.
> Use the present continuous for planned actions and events, usually in the very near future.
> Lauren _____ (have) dinner with her mother tonight.
> *Be going to* is used much more than *will* in conversation.

> Check your answers: Grammar reference, p. 110

6. Choose the best option.

1. Your bag looks heavy. Give it to me. I **will / am going to** help you carry it.
2. What **are you doing / will you do** this weekend? Do you have plans?
3. My friends can't go out tonight. They **will / are going to** study for the big math test.
4. What **are we having / will we have** for dinner tonight?
5. If all of you are going dancing now, I think I **will / am going to** go to bed. I'm tired.
6. Dave and Julianne **will / are going to** take a trip to Chile next year.

7. Complete the sentences with a verb from the box. Use *will* for first conditional sentences. For other sentences, use *be going to*.

go	see	study
get	stay	✓ take

1. I _am going to take_ an English course in New York next summer.
2. If my brother doesn't go to college, he _____ a job.
3. My best friend _____ harder next semester. Her grades are just terrible now.
4. If I don't have any plans this weekend, I _____ home and watch TV.
5. We _____ Julie tonight.
6. Your friends _____ to camp this summer.

> **First conditional**
> Use first conditional sentences to talk about things that may happen in the future.
> If you don't go to bed soon, you **will** be tired tomorrow.
> If you hurry up, we **will** have time to see a movie tonight.
> If you wear your boots, your feet **won't** get wet in the rain.

Speaking: *I'm going to . . .*

8. YOUR TURN Work with a partner. Ask and answer the questions.

1. What are you going to do when you finish high school?
2. What are you doing this weekend?

> What are you going to do when you finish high school?

> I think I'm going to go to college. But maybe I'll travel for a few months first.

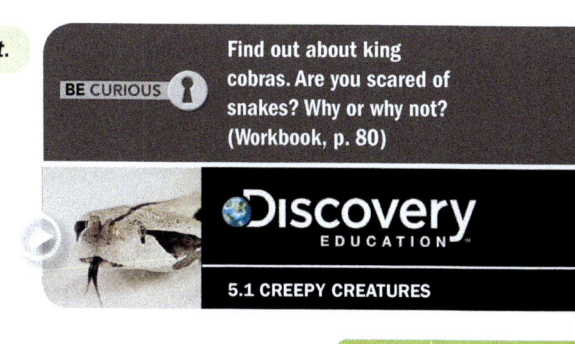

BE CURIOUS Find out about king cobras. Are you scared of snakes? Why or why not? (Workbook, p. 80)

Discovery EDUCATION

5.1 CREEPY CREATURES

Scared? I was TERRIFIED!

Listening: Conversations at an amusement park

1. Work with a partner. Look at the picture on the left. How do you think the people on the roller coaster feel? Do you like roller coasters? Why? / Why not?

2. Listen to two conversations between a group of friends at an amusement park. How do Alyssa and Bruno feel (a) at the beginning of the day, and (b) at the end of the day?

3. Listen again. Choose the correct answer to each question.
   Conversation 1:
   1. Which ride is Alyssa scared of?
      a. The Scream Machine   b. The Colossus   c. The Tidal Wave
   2. Why doesn't Bruno like the Tidal Wave?
      a. The line is short.   b. He doesn't like the water.   c. He wants to swim.
   3. Why does Colin suggest starting with The Scream Machine?
      a. The line is short.   b. It's very scary.   c. It's a lot of fun.

   Conversation 2:
   4. What was Colin's favorite ride?
      a. The Colossus   b. The Tidal Wave   c. The Scream Machine
   5. What was the problem at the end of the day?
      a. They missed the bus.   b. They spent a lot of money.   c. There's nothing to eat.

Vocabulary: -ed and -ing adjective endings

4. Look at the pictures and read the Notice it box. Circle the correct adjectives. Then listen and check your answers.
   1. The movie we saw last night was **terrified / terrifying**!
   2. Yesterday, we looked at the physics of roller coasters in class. It was very **interested / interesting**.
   3. I was completely **surprised / surprising** when I got the present you sent me.
   4. We went on a 20-kilometer walk in the country last weekend. It was **exhausted / exhausting**!
   5. I'm **confused / confusing**. Do we have a test tomorrow or not?
   6. My brother fell down in the cafeteria yesterday. Everyone saw him, and he felt really **embarrassed / embarrassing**.
   7. After a three-week vacation at the beach, I felt really **relaxed / relaxing**.
   8. Some reality shows on TV are really **disgusted / disgusting**.

5. **YOUR TURN** Write six true sentences about your feelings and beliefs using the cues below. Then tell your partner.

interested in	_____	is / are disgusting
embarrassed by	_____	is / are exhausting
terrified of	_____	is / are confusing

   NOTICE IT
   Use -ed adjective endings to say how you feel. Use -ing adjective endings to talk about something or someone that causes that feeling.

I was terrified.

The ride was terrifying.

Grammar: Modals of probability – *must, can't, may, might, could*

6. Complete the chart.

Use *must* for something you're almost certain of.	Use *can't* for something you believe is impossible.	Use *may, might,* and *could* for something that you believe is possible.
You have to be 14 or older to go on that ride. It _____ **be** really terrifying.	Ralph doesn't speak French, so he _____ **be** from France.	I don't know where your sister is, but she _____ **be** upstairs. I _____ **not go** to the barbecue because I haven't finished my homework. My dog doesn't want to eat. He _____ **be** sick.

> Check your answers: Grammar reference, p. 110

7. Choose the correct answers.

1. The roller coaster **must / can't** be fun. There are lots of people in line.
2. You **must / can't** expect to win the lottery. Millions of people play it every week.
3. You **must / can't** be really tired. You fell asleep twice during the movie.
4. My neighbor **must / can't** make a lot of money. He's always taking expensive trips.
5. She **must / can't** be a good student. She misses school at least once a week.
6. I **must / can't** be late. I left an hour early!

8. Complete the sentences with *must, can't,* or *could*.

1. You haven't eaten all day? Let me make you a snack. You _____ be hungry!
2. My mom _____ be at work or at the mall. She's not here.
3. We _____ fail the test. The teacher said we could look at our books.
4. Your brother _____ get hurt if he's not careful.
5. That guy over there is speaking French. He _____ be the new student from Canada.
6. You drank three glasses of water 15 minutes ago. You _____ be thirsty again.

> **Get it RIGHT!**
> Don't use *must* to discuss probability in the future.
> *If you don't go to bed now, you* **will** *be tired tomorrow.* NOT: *If you don't go to bed now, you* **must** *be tired tomorrow.*

Speaking: Surprising situations

9. YOUR TURN Read the situations below. Why do you think they're happening? Discuss with a partner. Be creative, and use *must, can't, might, may,* and *could*.

Situation 1: John bought a new bike last week, but he isn't using it. He's walking to school this morning.

Situation 2: Sean is a great athlete. He loves to play basketball, baseball, and football, but he isn't playing any sports at school this year.

Situation 3: Alicia has an important test in school tomorrow, but right now she's on a plane, going to Japan.

> John's bike must be broken.
>> It can't be broken. It's new.
>>> Well, it could have a flat tire. Maybe . . .

REAL TALK   5.2 WHAT ARE YOU AFRAID OF?

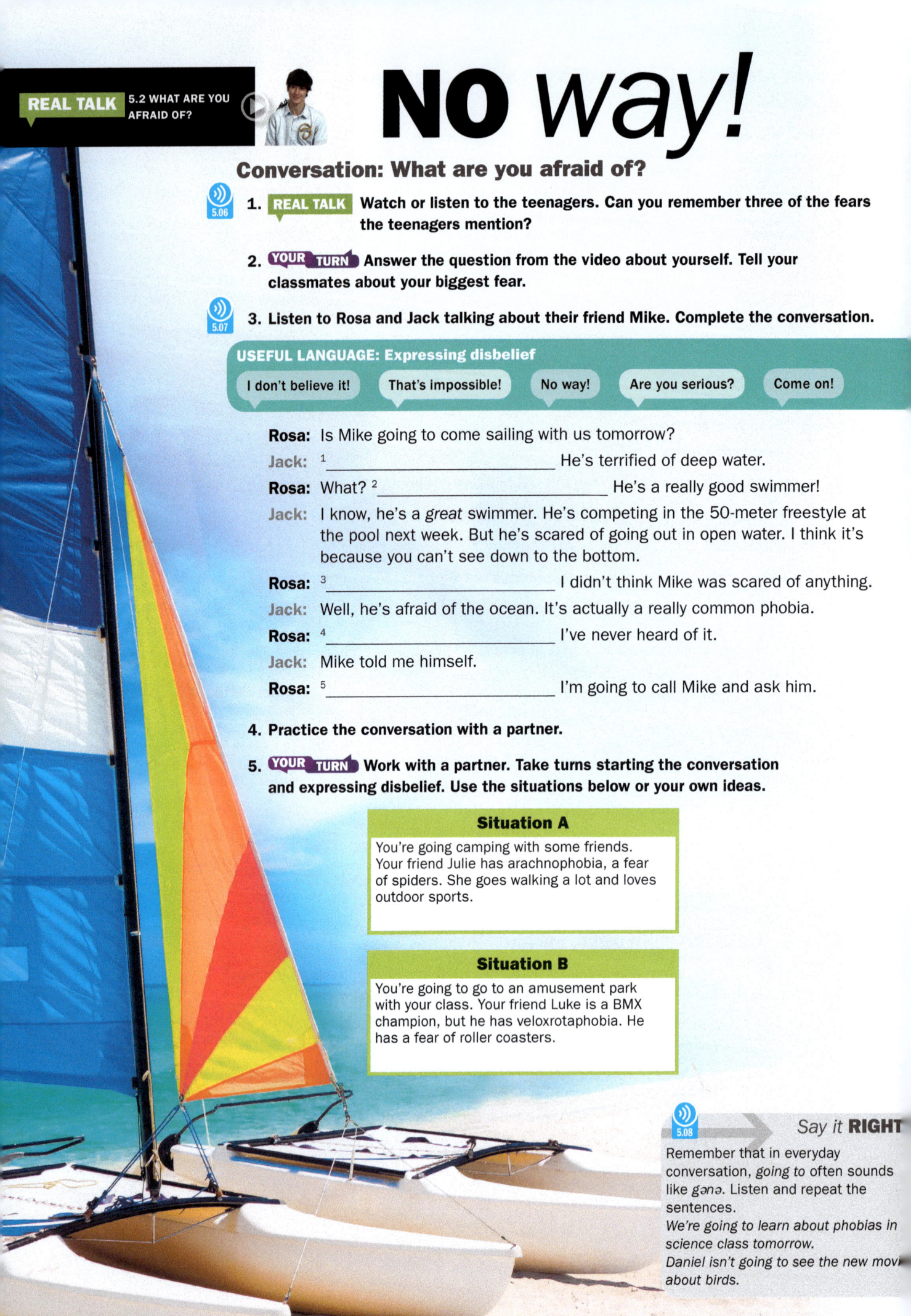

NO way!

Conversation: What are you afraid of?

1. **REAL TALK** Watch or listen to the teenagers. Can you remember three of the fears the teenagers mention?

2. **YOUR TURN** Answer the question from the video about yourself. Tell your classmates about your biggest fear.

3. Listen to Rosa and Jack talking about their friend Mike. Complete the conversation.

> **USEFUL LANGUAGE: Expressing disbelief**
> I don't believe it!   That's impossible!   No way!   Are you serious?   Come on!

Rosa: Is Mike going to come sailing with us tomorrow?

Jack: ¹_____ He's terrified of deep water.

Rosa: What? ²_____ He's a really good swimmer!

Jack: I know, he's a *great* swimmer. He's competing in the 50-meter freestyle at the pool next week. But he's scared of going out in open water. I think it's because you can't see down to the bottom.

Rosa: ³_____ I didn't think Mike was scared of anything.

Jack: Well, he's afraid of the ocean. It's actually a really common phobia.

Rosa: ⁴_____ I've never heard of it.

Jack: Mike told me himself.

Rosa: ⁵_____ I'm going to call Mike and ask him.

4. Practice the conversation with a partner.

5. **YOUR TURN** Work with a partner. Take turns starting the conversation and expressing disbelief. Use the situations below or your own ideas.

Situation A
You're going camping with some friends. Your friend Julie has arachnophobia, a fear of spiders. She goes walking a lot and loves outdoor sports.

Situation B
You're going to go to an amusement park with your class. Your friend Luke is a BMX champion, but he has veloxrotaphobia. He has a fear of roller coasters.

Say it RIGHT
Remember that in everyday conversation, *going to* often sounds like *gənə*. Listen and repeat the sentences.
We're going to learn about phobias in science class tomorrow.
Daniel isn't going to see the new movie about birds.

48 | Unit 5

To: Pete
From: Stefan
Subject: Afraid to fly!

Hi Pete,

Thanks for the email with your news. Now here's my news. Check this out: I'm going to stay with my cousins in Colorado this summer. I'm going with my parents, and the idea is that we'll all go camping together. It's really exciting, but the problem is that we're flying there ☹! I've never been on a plane before, and the truth is, I'm really worried about flying. I don't know what to do! When I think about getting on a plane, I feel tense and start sweating. It's embarrassing. Listen to this: I had to tell my mom, and she said it's just like going on a bus. She told me not to worry. Not very helpful! I want to go by car, but that will take four days. And so, the fact is, I might not go at all because I'm terrified of planes. What do you think I should do?

Sincerely,

Stefan

Reading to write: An email to a friend

6. Read Stefan's email. What is he worried about?

> ◉ *Focus on* **CONTENT**
> When you write an email about a problem, you can include this information:
> - A greeting *(Hi Mike! Dear Sandra,)*
> - Some personal news
> - What the problem is
> - How you feel about it and why
> - What you have / haven't done about it
> - A question to ask what your friend thinks

7. Read Stefan's email again. What information does he include for each category from the Focus on Content box?

> ◉ *Focus on* **LANGUAGE**
> **Introducing something**
> *Listen to this:*
> *The idea is (that) . . .*

8. Find examples of the items in the Focus on Language box in Stefan's email. Can you find two other ways of introducing information?

9. Rewrite the sentences using the words given.

1. We're going to Argentina next month. (listen to this)

   Listen to this: We're going to Argentina next month.

2. I'm going to get a dog. (check this out)

   _____

3. A lot of people have phobias about roller coasters. (the fact)

   _____

4. She doesn't want to go. (the truth)

   _____

Writing: An email to a friend about plans and problems

☐ **PLAN**
Think about a problem or worry you've had recently. It can be about anything: school, homework, your family, fears, phobias, or the future. Then think of someone you could send an email to for help with that problem. Look at the Focus on Content box and make notes about what you'll write.

☐ **WRITE**
Write your email. Use your notes and the language below to help you. Write about 120 words.

Thanks for your email / letter.

The idea is that . . .

It's really exciting / surprising / embarrassing . . .

I feel terrible / confused because . . .

What can I do? / What do you think I should do?

☐ **CHECK**
Check your writing. Can you answer "yes" to these questions?

- Is the information from the Focus on Content box in your email?
- Have you used expressions like *The problem is that* . . . in your email?

Superstitions? Who Needs Them?!

Many superstitions have been around for thousands of years. For example, some people believe that walking under ladders brings bad luck or finding a horseshoe brings good luck. Some superstitions began recently – for example, many soccer players don't change their socks or underwear while their team is winning.

Lots of people, however, believe strongly that superstitions are silly. They say that believing in superstitions is a way of trying to control things we can't control. They say that superstitions are based on old habits, old customs, and old beliefs. How is it possible that you could have bad luck by opening an umbrella inside a house? Why is the number 13 more dangerous than other numbers?

To prove their point, they have "Anti-Superstition Parties." These are usually held on a Friday the Thirteenth, a date that many people think brings bad luck. At these parties, people break mirrors, walk under ladders, and dance with open umbrellas. And nothing bad happens!

Alan Moore, a Chicago dentist, has gone to several anti-superstition parties. He said, "People must be crazy to believe that the number 7 is lucky or that they could be more successful by putting a horseshoe outside their house." Chelsea Evans, a chef from Dallas, agrees. "I love the parties. I've broken lots of mirrors and my life is going great!"

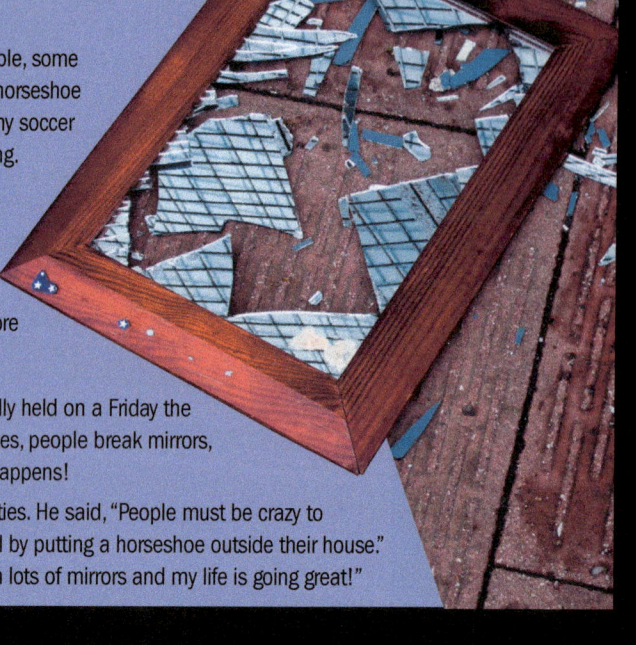

Culture: Anti-superstition parties

1. Read the title of the article and look at the picture. What do you think the article is about?

2. Read and listen to the article. Check (✓) the things you read and hear about.

   ☐ breaking mirrors   ☐ opening umbrellas
   ☐ black cats   ☐ walking under ladders
   ☐ blowing out birthday candles   ☐ throwing rice

3. Read the article again. Are the sentences below true (*T*) or false (*F*)?

   1. All superstitions have a recent origin. ____
   2. Some soccer players are superstitious. ____
   3. Lots of superstitions come from old habits and beliefs. ____
   4. At anti-superstition parties, people are careful to follow old superstitions. ____
   5. Alan and Chelsea are scared to go to anti-superstition parties. ____
   6. Chelsea's life is fine even though she has broken a lot of mirrors. ____

4. **YOUR TURN** Work with a partner. Ask and answer the questions.

   1. What superstitions exist in your country? Do you believe in any of them?
   2. Are there logical or scientific explanations for superstitions?
   3. Have you ever heard of anti-superstition parties? Would you like to go to one?

DID YOU KNOW…?
Fear of the number 13 is called triskaidekaphobia.

BE CURIOUS Find out about ancient Mayan calendars. What happened on Mayan "good days" and "bad days"? (Workbook, p. 81)

Discovery EDUCATION
5.3 CALENDARS OF THE ANCIENT MAYA

UNIT 5 REVIEW

Vocabulary

1. Write the common fears next to the words they are related to. There are two extra words.

birds	elevators	heights	snakes
clowns	✓ flying	insects	the dark

1. airplanes ___flying___
2. tall buildings _____
3. small spaces _____
4. poisonous animals _____
5. no light _____
6. spiders, beetles, butterflies _____

Grammar

2. Write sentences or questions with *be going to*. Use contracted forms if possible.

1. We / fly / to Japan / tomorrow
   We're going to fly to Japan tomorrow.
2. Jim / learn / the guitar / next semester
   _____
3. They / order / pizza / tonight
   _____
4. She / not use / her computer / this weekend
   _____
5. I / go to college / when I finish high school
   _____
6. Danielle / look for / a new job / next year
   _____

3. Complete the sentences with *must*, *can't*, or *might*.

1. Whose suitcase is that? It _____ belong to Erin, but I'm not sure.
2. I had my wallet just a second ago. It _____ be here somewhere.
3. Anna _____ be home sick. I saw her at school five minutes ago.
4. It's so cold outside that it _____ snow tonight.
5. You _____ be tired yet. We only started walking a few minutes ago.
6. Daniel isn't answering his phone. It _____ be turned off because he always answers it.

Useful language

4. Complete the conversation.

believe it	on
impossible	serious

Grace: We're going to an amusement park next weekend. Want to come?

Ryan: No, I'd better not. I always have bad luck when I go to amusement parks.

Grace: What do you mean?

Ryan: Every time I go, something bad happens. Last time, I was at the top of a roller coaster and the electricity went out. I sat in the car for 45 minutes.

Grace: Are you [1]_____?

Ryan: I'm not joking. And another time, I was on the Spinning Hat ride and the person next to me got sick. It was disgusting!

Grace: Come [2]_____. Just because you had a few bad things happen doesn't mean something bad will happen every time. That's [3]_____.

Ryan: No it isn't! And then, last summer, I went with my friends and fell down – I was just walking along – and had to go to the hospital!

Grace: I don't [4]_____!

Ryan: It's true! Sorry, but I think I'll just stay home.

PROGRESS CHECK: Now I can . . .

- ☐ identify and discuss common fears.
- ☐ talk about future events.
- ☐ talk about things that are possible and not possible.
- ☐ express disbelief.
- ☐ discuss superstitions.
- ☐ write an email to a friend about plans and problems.

CLIL PROJECT

5.4 CITY OR COUNTRY?, p. 118

Uncover Your Knowledge
UNITS 1–5 Review Game

TEAM 1 START

- Share an opinion with your teammate and ask him or her to agree with you. Your teammate disagrees with you and explains why.
- Tell your teammate about a time you felt embarrassed, stressed out, or wonderful.
- Say three future actions: one you've just decided to do, one for this weekend, and one for next year.
- Use each of these words in a unique sentence: terrified, interesting, confused, relaxing.
- Have your teammate tell you two things that are very surprising. Express your disbelief in two ways.
- Name the top three priorities you have in life, and explain why they are important to you.
- What do you have to do to get a good grade in English? Tell your teammate, using have to/don't have to.
- Give examples of three adventure travel activities you want to try.
- Role-play a conversation with your teammate. Invite him or her to an art exhibit and plan to meet.
- Say how long you've studied English. Then use a negative statement to tell your teammate the last time you saw a movie in a theater.
- Describe something you're looking forward to, something you want to find out about, and someplace you want to come back to.

Legend:
- GRAMMAR (green)
- VOCABULARY (blue)
- USEFUL LANGUAGE (orange)

TEAM 2
START

- Use the verbs *learn*, *play*, and *make* as the subjects of three different sentences.
- Name six basic needs that people have.
- Think about a few things you wanted to do last week. Use *already* to talk about something you did, and *yet* to talk about something you haven't done.
- How can you ask someone for information? Give three examples.
- Say two things you did yesterday and two things you used to do in the past but don't do anymore.
- In 30 seconds, name five things people are often afraid of.
- Say one thing you're almost sure about, one thing you think is possible, and one thing you believe is impossible. Use modals of probability.
- Give examples of five types of extreme weather.
- Tell your teammate something you hate doing, something you love doing, and something you don't mind doing.
- Name one type of artwork, one place to see art, and one type of artist.
- Role-play a conversation with your teammate. Ask him or her to help you with something.
- Tell your teammate that studying more would be a good thing for you to do. Say it three different ways, using modals of obligation.
- Imagine you are in a band. What instrument do you play? What other instruments do you have in the band? Give four examples.
- Tell your teammate two things you do every day and two things you are doing right now.

INSTRUCTIONS:

- Make teams and choose game pieces.
- Put your game pieces on your team's START.
- Flip a coin to see who goes first.
- Read the first challenge. Can you do it correctly?

  Yes ➔ Continue to the next challenge.

  No ➔ Lose your turn.

The first team to do all of the challenges wins!

Units 1–5 Review | 53

Simple present and present continuous review, page 5

Use the simple present to describe what normally happens. This includes routines and facts.	
It **sticks** to your face.	He/She/It **doesn't** live here.
I/You/We/They **like** cold weather.	I/You/We/They **don't like** hot weather.
I/You/We/They **get** home late.	I/You/We/They **don't go out** a lot.
Use the present continuous to describe something happening right now or these days.	
I'**m wearing** a hat.	I'**m not wearing** boots.
He/She **is working** right now.	He/She **isn't studying** right now.
You/We/They **are eating** hot food these days.	You/We/They **aren't drinking** coffee.

1. **Write sentences in the simple present or the present continuous.**

   1. it / always / rain / in April _____
   2. Tonya / write / a paper right now _____
   3. they / not walk / to work these days _____
   4. I / eat / dinner at 6:00 p.m. every night _____
   5. Jack / not like / subzero weather _____
   6. we / play / soccer outside right now _____

Simple past and past continuous review, page 7

Use the simple past to describe actions and events in the past.
I/You/He/She/We/They **took** a plane over part of Panama.
I/You/He/She/We/They **didn't have** to stop for food.
I/You/He/She/We/They **started** the trip in Alaska.
I/You/He/She/We/They **didn't start** the trip in California.
We **made** our own food.
He **didn't break** his arm, but it hurt a lot.
What **did** you **miss** the most?
Use the past continuous to describe actions and events in progress in the past.
I **was spending** the night in Quito when I heard that the road was closed.
He **wasn't wearing** a helmet when he fell.
We **were riding** through Colorado when Robert hurt his arm.
They **were eating** their lunch by the road when the storm started.
You **weren't talking** to me when I dropped my phone.
What **were** you **doing** last night when the electricity went out?

2. **Complete the sentences with the simple past or past continuous.**

   1. Jackie _____ (ride) her bike when she _____ (fall).
   2. We _____ (give) a lot of money to an education program last year.
   3. Paul and Oliver _____ (watch) TV when it _____ (start) to hail.
   4. I _____ (not study) when you _____ (call) me.
   5. My sisters _____ (not do) their homework when I _____ (get) home.
   6. She _____ (hear) about the blizzard at 10:00 a.m.

have to/don't have to, page 15

> Use have/has to to say that it is necessary to do something.
> Use don't/doesn't have to to say that it is not necessary to do something, but you can do it if you want to.

Affirmative	Negative
I/You/We/They **have to get** more sleep.	I/You/We/They **don't have to get up** early on Saturdays.
He/She **has to get up** early on Saturdays.	He/She **doesn't have to help** with the housework.

1. Write sentences with the correct form of *have to*. ✔ = yes, ✘ = no.

   1. I / have / more time for myself / ✔ _____
   2. Ben / help / around the house / ✔ _____
   3. Carol / shop / for clothes this weekend / ✘ _____
   4. They / get up / early tomorrow / ✔ _____
   5. You / work / late tonight / ✘ _____
   6. She / wash / the dishes / ✘ _____

Modals of obligation – *should, ought to, had better*, page 17

> Should, ought to, and had better have similar meanings. Use them to say what is a good or right thing to do.
> Use should and shouldn't for a personal opinion.
>
> I/You/He/She/We/They **should try** to work out more.
> I/You/He/She/We/They **shouldn't get** so stressed out.
>
> Use ought to and ought not to when you're talking about duty or the law.
>
> I/You/He/She/We/They **ought to call** the police about the car accident.
> I/You/He/She/We/They **ought not to enter** that part of the airport.
>
> Use had better and had better not to give very strong advice.
>
> I/You/He/She/We/They **had better start** studying now.
> I/You/He/She/We/They **had better not be** late for the test tomorrow.

2. Complete the sentences with the affirmative or negative of the word or phrase in parentheses.

   1. Kyle _____ relax. He's too stressed out about school. (should)
   2. You _____ apologize to Jenny. You made her feel terrible. (had better)
   3. Vic and Mary _____ go camping. They have a lot of homework this weekend. (should)
   4. We _____ tell your parents about what happened. They need to know. (ought to)
   5. They _____ take their cameras to the museum. You can't take photos there. (ought to)
   6. Jen _____ call Frank right now. He's at a job interview. (had better)

Verb + -ing form (gerund) review, page 25

We can use the -ing form of a verb after some verbs to talk about things we like or don't like.

Common verbs followed by -ing forms:
like, love, hate, enjoy, (not) mind

	-ing form		
I/You/We/They	love	drawing	pictures in my free time.
	don't like	going	to museums.
He/She	enjoys	looking	at sculptures.
	hates	helping	around the house.
	doesn't mind	doing	housework.

1. **Complete the conversations with the correct form of the verbs in the box.**

   don't like / go   enjoy / meet   hate / do   love / work   not mind / look

   1. **A:** Does your brother like art?
      B: Not really, but he _____ at murals.
   2. **A:** Who washes the dishes at your house?
      B: I do. And I _____ it!
   3. **A:** How is your brother's new job?
      B: Great. He _____ at the pizza place.
   4. **A:** Did you see the new sculpture at the museum?
      B: No, I didn't. I _____ to museums.
   5. **A:** Isn't your mother an artist? Could you introduce me to her?
      B: Sure. She _____ new people.

-ing forms (gerunds) as subjects, page 27

You can use the -ing form as the subject of a sentence. The verb is singular.

Playing several instruments at once <u>takes</u> a lot of energy.

Singing at the same time I play instruments <u>is</u> hard.

Being here at the festival <u>is</u> really special to me.

For the negative, use not before the -ing form.

Not enjoying some kinds of music <u>is</u> normal.

Not playing music <u>makes</u> me sad.

2. **Put the words in the correct order to make sentences.**

   1. is / the trumpet / playing / difficult
      _____
   2. me into trouble / practicing / the piano / gets / not
      _____
   3. easy / finding / isn't / a good keyboard player
      _____
   4. before a concert / it hard to play the flute / makes / eating
      _____
   5. getting / ruins / a good night's sleep / not / my day
      _____

Present perfect with *already*, *yet*, and *just*, page 35

We can use already *in affirmative sentences in the present perfect.*

I/You/We/They **have already been** at sea for four days.

He/She **has already cooked** three meals for the others on the ship.

The ship/It **has already left** the port.

We can use yet *in negative sentences in the present perfect.*

I/You/We/They **haven't found** turtles **yet**.

He/She **hasn't visited** the ship **yet**.

It **hasn't rained yet**.

Use just *with the present perfect to say that something happened very recently.*

I/You/We/They **have just seen** dolphins.

He/She **has just boarded** the ship.

It **has just gotten** dark.

1. Circle the correct words to complete the sentences.

    1. Donna has **just** / **yet** bought a mountain bike.
    2. I've **already** / **yet** gone sailing twice this summer.
    3. Carlos and Doug haven't left for summer camp **just** / **yet**.
    4. She hasn't gone on a safari **already** / **yet**.
    5. We've **already** / **just** packed our suitcases for the cruise. We packed them a week ago!
    6. It has **just** / **yet** started raining, so we can't go ballooning now.

Present perfect with *for* and *since*, page 37

Use the present perfect with for *or* since *for past actions and events continuing into the present.*

Use for *with a period of time such as* a week, two months, *or* five years.

I/You/We/They **have been** here **for** three days.

I/You/We/They **haven't seen** Tom **for** three days.

He/She **has worked** at the rafting company **for** a month.

He/She **hasn't gone** on a trip **for** two years.

Use since *with a specific date or time.*

I/You/We/They **have been** here **since** last Wednesday.

I/You/We/They **haven't taken** a vacation **since** last June.

He/She **has lived** in Colorado **since** 2010.

He/She **hasn't called** me **since** last Monday.

2. Complete the sentences with the present perfect of the verbs in parentheses and *for* or *since*.

    1. Mario _____ (known) Josh _____ two years.
    2. Ken and Lisa _____ (not eat) _____ 8:00 a.m.
    3. We _____ (wait) for Cindy _____ an hour.
    4. I _____ (live) in Mexico _____ 2008.
    5. You _____ (not see) me _____ three weeks.

Future review – will, be going to, present continuous, page 45

Use will, be going to, and the present continuous to talk about the future.
Use will for actions and events that we decide to do in the moment of speaking.

Are you going running now? I **will go** with you.
I/You/He/She/We/They **will go** to the park.
I/You/He/She/We/They **won't go** to the store.

Use going to for planned actions and events. They may be in the near future or in a more distant future time.

I'm **(not) going to share** a room with other students.
He/She **is (not) going to fly** to Las Vegas next month.
You/We/They **are (not) going to be** in different schools next year.

Use the present continuous for planned actions and events, usually in the very near future.

I **am (not) traveling** to New York soon.
He/She **is (not) having** dinner with her mother tonight.
You/We/They **are (not) going** to the wedding tomorrow.

Be going to is used much more than will in conversation.

1. **Complete the sentences with the given form of the verbs in parentheses.**

   1. Kendra _____ a test tomorrow. (take – present continuous)
   2. Wait for me! I _____ ready in five minutes. (be – *will*)
   3. Sally and Mark _____ a movie tonight. (not see – *going to*)
   4. He _____ to Rio de Janeiro tonight. (not fly – present continuous)
   5. My cousins _____ me at the circus on Friday. (meet – *going to*)

Modals of probability – must, can't, may, might, could, page 47

Use must for something you're almost certain of.
Use can't for something you believe is impossible.
Use might, may, and could for something that you believe is possible.

I/You/He/She/It/We/They	**must be** really terrifying.
	must be terrified.
	must not be relaxed.
	can't be from France.
	may/might/could be upstairs.
	may/might not go to the barbecue.
	may/might/could be sick.

2. **Circle the correct answer. Sometimes more than one answer is possible.**

   1. I ____ be in class tomorrow. I don't feel well.
      a. could   b. might not   c. must   d. may not

   2. You ____ be exhausted. You only slept an hour last night.
      a. can't   b. must not   c. must   d. might not

   3. Eva ____ be confused about our homework. She just explained it to me.
      a. can't   b. could   c. may   d. might not

   4. We ____ go on the roller coaster. I don't think we're tall enough.
      a. must   b. might not   c. may not   d. could

   5. They ____ be surprised. They knew we were planning a party.
      a. could   b. may   c. can't   d. might

This page intentionally left blank.

CLIL PROJECT

The San PEOPLE

1. Label the pictures with the correct words.

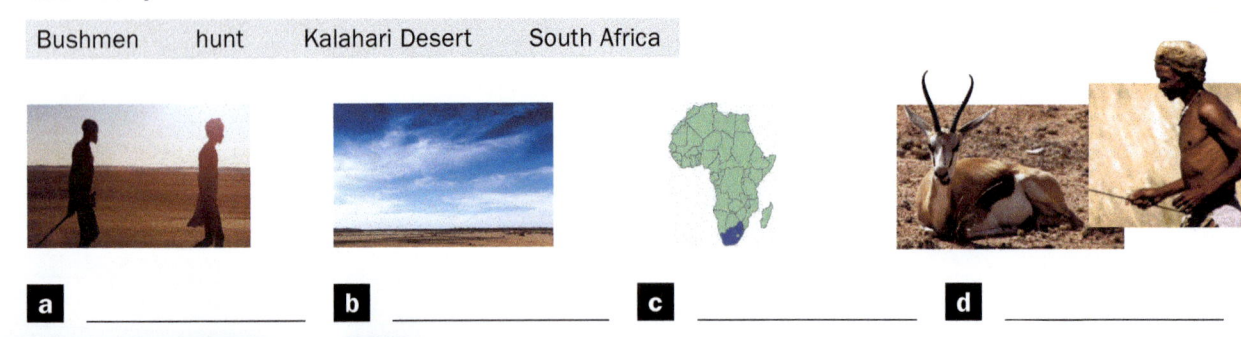

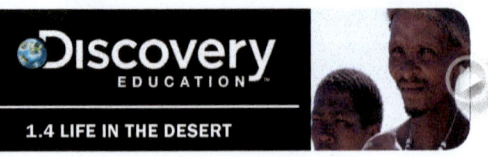

Bushmen   hunt   Kalahari Desert   South Africa

a _____   b _____   c _____   d _____

Discovery EDUCATION
1.4 LIFE IN THE DESERT

2. Watch the video. Complete the phrases with the correct adjectives.

animal   bright   difficult   high   young

1. _____ temperatures
2. a _____ place to live
3. a _____ future
4. _____ tracks
5. a _____ springbok

3. Match the phrases to make sentences.

1. The Kalahari Desert ____
2. The San people have lived ____
3. Recently the South African government ____
4. They get their food ____
5. From the footprints, ____

a. from plants and animals.
b. Isaac can tell the size of the animal.
c. in the Kalahari for thousands of years.
d. is a place of high temperatures and little rain.
e. gave a part of the Kalahari to the Khomani San.

PROJECT Learn about a group of people who live close to nature. Some choices are: the Inuit, the Saami, Australian Aborigines, or native South Americans in the Amazon rain forest. Find out more about them and answer the questions below. Present your information to the class.

- What is their name?
- Where do they live?
- What kinds of food are popular in the region?
- How do they get food?
- What kinds of animals live in the region?
- What are some difficulties of living in the region?
- What festivals or celebrations do they have?
- How is their life changing?

Renaissance GREATS

1. Label the pictures with the correct words.

| architecture | astronomy | the Medicis | perspective | three-dimensional |

a _____ b _____ c _____ d _____ e _____

2. Watch the video. Put the sentences 1–6 in the correct categories.

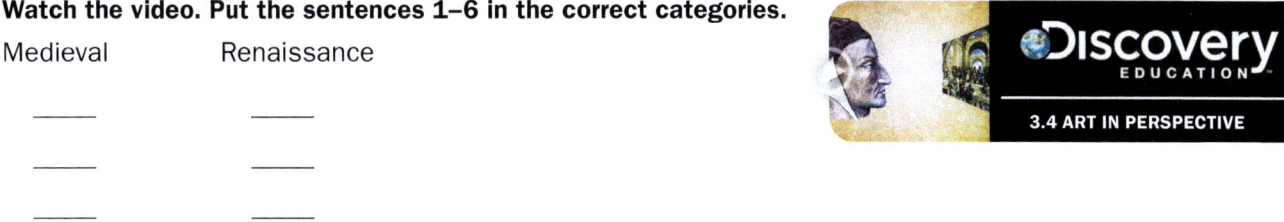

Medieval   Renaissance

____   ____

____   ____

____   ____

1. Paintings didn't look realistic.
2. Rich families gave a lot of money to artists.
3. Paintings looked flat.
4. More important things were bigger in paintings.
5. Paintings were as realistic as possible.
6. Paintings looked three-dimensional.

Discovery EDUCATION
3.4 ART IN PERSPECTIVE

3. Complete the paragraph with the correct words.

| created | painters | painting | perspective | realistic |

Across Europe, ¹_____ began to use ²_____ in their work. Filippo Brunelleschi was the first Italian to do this. He ³_____ a ⁴_____ of this building that looked exactly like the real thing. This was the beginning of ⁵_____ art.

PROJECT

Leonardo da Vinci, Michelangelo, Filippo Brunelleschi – these are three great artists of the Renaissance. Choose one of them, or think of another, and make a poster. Include the following information on your poster, and then present to your class.

- A picture of your artist
- The years they lived
- Two interesting facts about their life
- A picture of a painting or a building they created
- Describe two things they painted, built, created, or discovered

CLIL PROJECT

Guided TOURS

1. **Which sentences are true about living in the city? Which sentences are true about the country? Label the sentences *city* or *country*.**

   1. There are more things to do, during the day and at night. _____
   2. You can enjoy the beauties of nature. _____
   3. The streets can be crowded and noisy. _____
   4. Sometimes people try to steal your money. _____
   5. You know your neighbors and other people. _____
   6. People are friendlier and say hello to you. _____
   7. Places like schools and hospitals are closer to your home. _____

Discovery EDUCATION
5.4 CITY OR COUNTRY?

2. **Watch the video. Complete the sentences with the correct words.**

   | big | cultural | fashionable | freezing | quiet | small | stylish |

   1. In Russia, many people live in the countryside or in _____ towns.
   2. But recently, more and more people are moving from the countryside to _____ cities.
   3. There are _____ shops and _____ restaurants.
   4. But there are some _____ places in cities.
   5. In Moscow, people can relax by the river – even in the _____ months of winter.
   6. _____ events bring people together.

PROJECT
Write a guide to your city or town. Tell visitors what's different about your part of the world. Use the questions below.

Why go? Give three reasons.
_____

How do you get there? Describe the best routes by plane, train, bus, and car.
_____

What can you see? Name three things.
_____

What can you do? Describe two activities.
_____

Uncover 3 Combo A

Kathryn O'Dell

Workbook

CAMBRIDGE UNIVERSITY PRESS

Discovery EDUCATION

Life on the Edge

VOCABULARY Extreme weather

1. Complete the sentences and the crossword.

ACROSS

2. We didn't go for a boat ride because of high ____winds____.

4. There was a lot of _____ and lightning during the storm.

6. We couldn't see the road very well because of the _____. It was very thick.

7. It started to _____ during the storm. We were afraid the windows might break from the ice.

DOWN

1. I didn't have school today because of the _____.

3. It was over 35°C during the _____ wave.

5. The game was canceled because of _____ rain.

2. Complete the weather report with words and phrases from Exercise 1.

Worldwide Weather

There is a ¹ ____blizzard____ in Anchorage, Alaska, today. Expect 25 to 50 centimeters of snow by the end of the day. ² _____ of 80 kilometers per hour are blowing the snow around.

³ _____ is coming down quickly in several cities in southern Germany. Falling ice can damage cars and hurt people.

Today in Mexico City there is ⁴ _____ falling at about 3 centimeters per hour. Right now, it's quiet, but expect ⁵ _____ at night.

The Golden Gate Bridge is closed in San Francisco because of ⁶ _____. Drivers can't see very far in front of them. Be careful on the roads.

There is a ⁷ _____ in Dubai with temperatures over 40°C.

3. What kinds of extreme weather do you think can happen in these places?

1.  ____high winds,_____

2. _____

3. _____

GRAMMAR Present tense review – simple present and present continuous

1 Look at Eva's weekend schedule. Complete the sentences about her routine with the simple present forms of the verbs.

Friday	Saturday	Sunday
go to class	work at food court	visit grandparents
study with Kyle at library	hang out with friends	make lunch with grandma

1. Eva ____goes____ to class on Fridays. She ____doesn't go____ to class on Saturdays and Sundays.
2. Eva and Kyle _____ at Eva's house. They _____ at the library.
3. Eva _____ at the food court on Saturdays. She _____ at the bike shop.
4. Eva and her friends _____ after work.
5. Eva _____ her grandparents on Sundays.
6. Eva and her grandma _____ lunch. Her grandpa _____ lunch.

2 Put the words in the correct order to make sentences. Change the verbs to the present continuous.

1. right / the snow / now / melt
   The snow is melting right now.
2. fly / Jake / to Alaska
   _____
3. in the park / play / they / basketball
   _____
4. my / I / skateboard / not ride
   _____
5. vacation / plan / a / we
   _____
6. and Tara / coats / not wear / Ed
   _____

3 Check (✓) if the activities are routines or happening right now.

	Routine	Right now
1. I'm driving in a blizzard.		✓
2. Dennis goes to the beach with his friends.		
3. Sarah drives to class.		
4. You aren't visiting your cousins.		
5. We are going to the beach with our friends.		
6. Mark and Penny visit their grandparents.		

4 Complete the conversation with the simple present or present continuous forms of the verbs.

Tina: Hi, Leo. What are you doing these days?

Leo: I ¹____am taking____ (take) a class at the community center, and I ²_____ (play) on a new soccer team. I ³_____ (be) really busy.

Tina: What class?

Leo: It ⁴_____ (be) a meteorology class. You know, a class about weather.

Tina: I see. What are you studying?

Leo: Well, right now, we ⁵_____ (learn) about weather changes around the world.

Tina: That sounds interesting.

Leo: Yeah. The weather ⁶_____ (change) a lot these days. I ⁷_____ (read) a chapter about extreme weather right now.

Tina: Speaking of weather, I have to go! It ⁸_____ (start) to rain.

Leo: Oh, no. I guess I ⁹_____ (not go) to my soccer game now. We ¹⁰_____ (play) at the park every Tuesday, but we ¹¹_____ (not go) when it rains!

VOCABULARY Basic needs

1 Label the pictures with the correct words.

clothes	health care
communication	a home
education	money
entertainment	transportation
✓ food and drink	

1. _food and drink_
2. _____ 
3. _____ 
4. _____ 
5. _____ 
6. _____ 
7. _____ 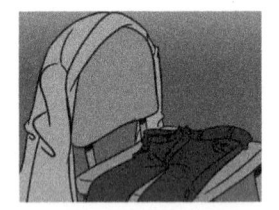
8. _____ 
9. _____ 

2 Complete the sentence with the words and phrases from Exercise 1.

1. My cousin wants to buy _a home_ in our neighborhood, but he doesn't have enough _____ yet.
2. There are many _____ options in this city – buses, trains, and subways.
3. I'm getting a good _____ at Clinton High School.
4. I need to buy some new _____ for school.
5. Texting is a more popular form of _____ than talking on the phone for teens.
6. Do you go to the movies for _____?
7. You can get _____ at the food court in the mall.
8. My parents have good _____. Their doctor is excellent.

3 Answer the questions with your own information.

1. What do you usually do for entertainment?

   I usually watch movies on my computer.
   _____

2. How much money do you spend every week?

   _____
   _____

3. What form of transportation do you use to get to school?

   _____
   _____

4. What is the main form of communication you use with your friends?

   _____
   _____

5. What kind of clothes do you like to wear?

   _____
   _____

GRAMMAR Past tense review – simple past and past continuous

1 Write sentences with the simple past.

1. Larry / get / home late last night
   Larry got home late last night.
2. We / not go / to the concert
   _____
3. I / send / Jen three text messages
   _____
4. They / ride / their skateboards to school
   _____
5. You / not call / last night
   _____
6. Sandra / wear / jeans to school
   _____
7. I / not be / at school yesterday
   _____
8. My cousin / arrive / from Argentina last night
   _____

2 Complete the sentences with the past continuous forms of the verbs.

1. Laura ____*was studying*____ (study) during the blizzard.
2. Vic and Dan _____ (ride) the bus together.
3. We _____ (not walk) outside when it started to hail.
4. I _____ (not wear) a coat when it got cold.
5. You _____ (shop) when I called you.
6. Frank _____ (wear) a helmet when he fell off his bike.

3 Complete the sentences with the simple past or past continuous forms of the verbs.

1. I ____*didn't watch*____ (not watch) the news last night. I was too busy!
2. Torrey _____ (see) the tornado before it hit the town.
3. I put on a hat, but the wind _____ (blow) it off my head.
4. Jess _____ (not wear) a raincoat when the rain came, so she got really wet.
5. Sam _____ (listen) to the radio when he heard the weather report.
6. Reggie _____ (not be) afraid of storms until he experienced high winds.

4 Correct the sentences and questions.

1. Marcos ~~use~~ *used* to play in the snow.
2. We use drive to California every summer.
3. Rita not used to take the bus to school.
4. Did you used to camp in the mountains?
5. I used to bought new clothes at the mall.
6. Jack and Paul use to watch TV on Saturday mornings.

5 Complete the text with the simple past, past continuous, or *used to*.

On the Edge

Tonya Harris lives on the edge – on the edge of a mountain! One time, she and her younger brother ¹ ____*were playing*____ (play) soccer outside when her brother ² _____ (kick) the ball off the mountain. He ³ _____ (chase) the ball when Tonya ⁴ _____ (scream). She ⁵ _____ (stop) him from going over the edge of the mountain. Now that her brother is older, she doesn't worry about him, but she ⁶ _____ (worry) about him all the time!

Tonya's school is at the bottom of the mountain. When she was young, she ⁷ _____ (take) the bus to school, but now she rides her bike. Yesterday, she ⁸ _____ (ride) her bike when she ⁹ _____ (fall). She ¹⁰ _____ (break) her arm. Her parents ¹¹ _____ (drive) to work when they ¹² _____ (see) her. They ¹³ _____ (take) her to the doctor right away. Tonya ¹⁴ _____ (not go) to school yesterday. This morning, Tonya ¹⁵ _____ (go) back to school. While her friends ¹⁶ _____ (wait) for class to start, they ¹⁷ _____ (write) their names on her cast. Tonya likes her life on the edge of the mountain, but she's going to be more careful!

CONVERSATION Agreeing and disagreeing

1. Circle the correct answers.

1. **A:** This weather is crazy, ____?
   B: Yeah. It's an incredible blizzard.
   a. don't you think   b. I disagree

2. **A:** Do you think it's going to snow more?
   B: ____. I think the blizzard is over.
   a. I disagree   b. I don't think so

3. **A:** I hate winter weather.
   B: ____. I love the snow!
   a. See what I mean   b. I disagree

4. **A:** The snow is so high!
   B: ____? I told you it was 30 centimeters!
   a. See what I mean   b. I don't think so

5. **A:** I can't wait for spring. ____?
   B: Actually, I like the winter.
   a. Don't you agree   b. See what I mean

2 Circle the correct phrases.

Tim: Can you believe this blizzard? It's the biggest one so far this year, [1]**I don't think so / don't you think**?

Donna: Yes, I think you're right. There's at least 30 centimeters of snow on the ground! It'd be better to live somewhere warm. [2]**Don't you agree / I disagree**?

Tim: [3]**See what I mean / I don't think so**. I really like the cold weather.

Donna: Really? I prefer a warmer place. There's so much more to do in warm weather!

Tim: [4]**I disagree / Don't you agree**! I do a lot in the winter. There are so many winter activities here – like snowboarding and skiing.

Donna: We did have fun on the ski trip last weekend.

Tim: [5]**I don't think so / See what I mean**? Winter is great.

Donna: Yeah, I guess so. But this blizzard is terrible! It's too cold to ski or snowboard.

Tim: That's true.

READING TO WRITE

1 Number the parts of a persuasive email in order from 1–3.

_____ Explain why you think your readers should do what you're suggesting.

_____ State your position again in a different way.

_____ State your position on a topic.

2 Circle the correct words.

To: martin@net.cup.org
From: lydia@net.cup.org
Subject: Cuernavaca is the best!

Hi Martin,
I'm living in Cuernavaca in Mexico now. I love it. I think it's the best city in Mexico!
¹**First of all** / **Second**, it's like spring all year. ²**The best part** / **For example**, there are a lot of flowers and plants everywhere – all year long.
³**For example** / **Second**, there's a lot to do and see in Cuernavaca. ⁴**For instance** / **First of all**, there are historic buildings, carnivals, and a lot of markets.
⁵**The best part** / **For example** is the people. There are many places to meet friends. I met two new friends at the skate park yesterday!
Cuernavaca really is a great place to live. I hope you can visit me this year.
Your cousin,
Lydia

---

3 Match the sentences. Then write them in the correct places in the email.

1. The best part is all of the places to eat. _____
2. First of all, there are many things to do outside. _____
3. Second, there are many things to do inside. _____

a. For example, you can go to sports events and parks.
b. For instance, there are many museums in Chicago.
c. Chicago has food from all over the world!

To: evelyn@net.cup.org
From: talia@net.cup.org
Subject: Come to Chicago!

Hi Evelyn,
I want you to come visit me in Chicago on your school break! Chicago is one of the best cities to visit.

_____
_____
_____
_____
_____
_____

So please come visit me. We'll have lots of fun!
Your friend,
Talia

2 First Things First!

VOCABULARY Priorities

1 Put the words in the correct order to make phrases about priorities.

1. out / working

   working out

2. out / weekend / on / staying / the / late

   _____

3. with / hanging / friends / out

   _____

4. clothes / for / shopping

   _____

5. the / helping / house / around

   _____

6. something / doing / creative

   _____

7. for / time / having / yourself

   _____

8. friends / online / chatting / with

   _____

9. enough / sleep / getting

   _____

2 What are the people doing? Write sentences using eight of the phrases from Exercise 1.

1. Carol is communicating with Jim and Vicky on her computer.

   She's chatting with friends online.

2. Brad went to bed at 9:00 p.m. last night. It's 8:00 a.m., and he's still in bed.

   _____

3. Jenny and Mark are exercising at the gym.

   _____

4. Mandy is looking at T-shirts and jeans.

   _____

5. Trent and Sue are cleaning the kitchen and washing clothes.

   _____

6. It's Saturday at 11:00 p.m. Wendy is at a concert.

   _____

7. Carlos is talking at a café with Luke, Dana, and Cindy.

   _____

8. Luisa is painting a picture.

   _____

3 Answer the questions with your own information.

1. What do you do when you have time for yourself?

   When I have time for myself, I read in the park.

2. How late do you stay out on the weekends?

   _____

3. Where do you hang out with friends? What do you do?

   _____

4. Do you help around the house? What do you do?

   _____

5. Do you like shopping for clothes? Where do you go?

   _____

8 | Unit 2

GRAMMAR have to/don't have to; must

1 Look at Matt and Carrie's To Do list and write sentences about their chores. ✓ = *have to*, ✗ = *not have to*.

To Do Weekend chores and activities		
Matt	**Carrie**	**Both**
shop for clothes ✓	work out ✗	help around the house ✓
fix the computer ✓	practice the piano ✓	work in the yard ✗
go to soccer practice ✗	take the dog for a walk ✓	do homework ✓

1. *Matt has to shop for clothes.*
2. _____
3. _____
4. _____
5. _____
6. _____
7. _____
8. _____
9. _____

2 Write sentences about the skate park rules with *must* and *must not*.

Do . . .	Don't . . .
• wear a helmet • take turns on the ramps • throw away trash	• bring food or drink into the skate area • use the park after 9:00 p.m. • ride bikes on the ramps

1. *You must wear a helmet.*
2. _____
3. _____
4. _____
5. _____
6. _____

3 Write two sentences for each picture with the words from the box and the correct form of (*not*) *have to* or *must* (*not*).

> you / turn off / your phone
> she / call / her mother now
> you / use / your phone
> she / call / her mother later

1. _____
2. _____

3. _____
4. _____

4 Write sentences about your chores with (*not*) *have to*.

Have to
1. *I have to wash the dishes.*
2. _____
3. _____
Don't have to
4. _____
5. _____
6. _____

5 Write sentences about rules for a library with *must* (*not*).

Dos
1. _____
2. _____
Don'ts
3. *You must not run in the library.*
4. _____

VOCABULARY Emotions

1 Find six more words for emotions.

S	H	I	O	H	P	R	O	F	G	W	U	M	K	P
T	B	S	P	Z	J	X	G	V	R	Q	I	A	Q	N
R	R	L	R	N	B	A	A	W	F	U	L	W	C	Z
E	M	I	O	M	D	D	Y	B	N	A	T	O	E	F
S	L	U	U	I	G	Z	K	P	D	Y	N	N	X	V
S	Z	U	D	U	N	A	W	E	P	G	E	D	H	L
E	M	B	A	R	R	A	S	S	E	D	R	E	A	B
D	I	S	U	R	H	I	Q	U	R	B	A	R	U	D
O	F	Z	S	C	K	R	J	G	E	F	P	F	S	P
U	E	T	E	R	R	I	F	I	E	D	K	U	T	M
T	H	W	N	N	X	H	T	S	T	M	H	L	E	O
G	V	K	A	S	L	S	T	P	R	H	X	E	D	T

2 Complete the sentences with the correct words.

awful
embarrassed
exhausted
proud
✓ stressed out
terrified
wonderful

I have so much to do this week. I'm really
¹ _stressed out_ ! First of all, I have to give a speech in my class on Friday. I'm
² _____ because I really don't like speaking in front of people. I worked on the speech for hours last night, and today I'm
³ _____. Last time I gave a speech, I was so ⁴ _____ because I forgot what to say. It was
⁵ _____! But I'm going to practice a lot this time. I hope it's going to be
⁶ _____. I want to make my parents ⁷ _____.

3 How do you think the people feel in these situations? Use some of the words from Exercise 2. Sometimes more than one answer is possible.

1. John forgot his teacher's name. _embarrassed_
2. Linda is scared of spiders, and there is a huge one under her bed. _____
3. Abby has three tests tomorrow, and she has to take care of her younger brothers tonight. _____
4. Oliver's sister scored three goals in a soccer game. _____
5. Danny didn't get enough sleep last night. _____

4 How do you feel in these situations? Use words from Exercise 2.

1. You did well on a test. _____
2. You're riding a roller coaster. _____
3. You have to give a speech. _____
4. Your friend won an award. _____

GRAMMAR Modals of obligation – *should, ought to, had better*

1 Complete the advice with *should* (*not*) and the verbs.

Mike G My friends are going sky diving tomorrow, but I don't want to go. I'm terrified! What should I do?

Sara Li You ¹_____ (be) embarrassed. It's OK if you don't want to go.

Dave I agree. You ²_____ (tell) your friends you don't want to go.

Paula S I disagree. You ³_____ (try) it. It might be really fun!

Steven You ⁴_____ (go) with them on the plane. It will be fun. But, if you get scared, you ⁵_____ (jump). You ⁶_____ (do) anything that you don't want to do. You can decide when you get there.

2 Look at the pictures and complete the sentences with *ought (not) to* and the correct verbs.

No Parking

1. We ___ought not to park___ here.

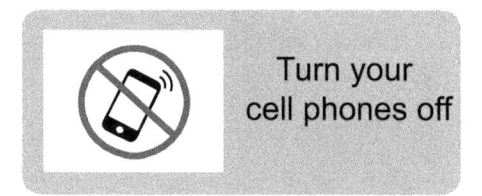

Turn your cell phones off

2. You _____ your cell phone off.

You can't take big bags on the plane

3. I _____ this bag on the plane. I'll have to check it.

Please be quiet

4. You _____ quiet in the library.

Don't sit on the grass

5. They _____ on the grass in the park.

3 Write sentences with *had better (not)*. ✓ = yes, ✗ = no.

1. Terry / hang out / with his friends tonight / ✗

   Terry had better not hang out with his friends tonight.

2. Josh and Mia / shop / for clothes before school starts / ✓

   _____

3. We / get / home on time / ✓

   _____

4. You / chat / online very long / ✗

   _____

5. Serena / help / around the house / ✓

   _____

6. I / get / too stressed out / ✗

   _____

It's + adjective + infinitive

4 Correct the sentences.

   It's
1. ~~It~~ easy to be proud of your friends.
2. It's no difficult to ride a bike.
3. You shouldn't to stay out late.
4. It's important have time for yourself.
5. It fun not to shop for clothes.
6. You ought call the police about the robbery.
7. It's important is quiet in the library.
8. You had better to get enough sleep.

5 Read the sentences. Then write sentences with similar meanings with the modals.

1. It's a good idea for John to work out. (should)

   John should work out.

2. My cousin needs to call me. (had better)

   _____

3. You can't drive on that side of the road. (ought not to)

   _____

4. We can't stay out too late. (had better not)

   _____

5. It's required that I buy a ticket before I get on the bus. (ought to)

   _____

6. It's a bad idea for Lori to chat online with her friends for hours. (shouldn't)

   _____

CONVERSATION: Helping someone to do something

1 Put the words in order to make sentences.

1. show / let / you / me
   Let me show you.

2. at / very / that / I'm / like / not / good / things
   _____

3. if / you / like / I'll / give / a hand / you
   _____

4. really / simple / it's / pretty
   _____

5. not / how / it / I'm / sure / to do
   _____

2 Complete the conversation with the sentences from Exercise 1.

Sam: Hey, Dee.

Dee: Hi, Sam. It looks like you're having problems with your phone.
¹ *I'll give you a hand if you like.*

Sam: That'd be great. I need to get my email on my phone, but
² _____
Do you know how?

Dee: Yeah, I do. I just did it with my new phone last week.
³ _____

Sam: Well, you might think it's easy, but
⁴ _____
I'm really terrible with technology.

Dee: It's really not difficult to do.
⁵ _____
You'll see.

Sam: OK. Thanks.

Dee: So, first, go to "Settings" and click on "Email." Then click on "Add account" and enter your email address.

Sam: Wow. That *was* easy. Thanks.

READING TO WRITE

1 Complete Lucas's blog post with *a few*, *a little*, *too many*, or *too much*.

Last month, I was really stressed out. I was involved in ¹ __too many__ activities. I was taking three classes, working part-time at the mall, working out at the gym, and playing on a soccer team. I was doing ² _____! I only had ³ _____ time to hang out with my friends. At the end of the week, I was exhausted, and I really missed my friends.

I made some changes in my lifestyle. I made sure that I had ⁴ _____ minutes for myself each day. Every morning, I read before breakfast, and at night, I took ⁵ _____ time to play video games. I also made sure I was getting enough sleep. Then I started doing some of my needed activities with friends. I started working out with ⁶ _____ friends and studying for my classes with my best friend. I still have ⁷ _____ to do, but at least I'm seeing my friends more!

2 Read Lucas's blog post again. Answer the questions.

1. What was Lucas's problem?
   _____

2. What four things caused his problem?
   _____
   _____
   _____

3. What three steps did Lucas take to solve his problem?
   _____
   _____
   _____

3 Read Lucas's blog post again. Check (✓) the advice he would give other people.

If you are involved in too many activities, . . .

☑ you have to have time for yourself.
☐ you shouldn't work out.
☐ you should try to do some of your activities with other people.
☐ you can study with friends.
☐ you shouldn't study so much.
☐ you had better quit your job.
☐ you should sleep less to make time to get all of your work done.
☐ you ought to get enough sleep.

4 Complete the end of Lucas's blog post with the phrases you checked in Exercise 3.

If you're like me and are involved in too many activities, I have some advice for you. ¹ *You have to have time for yourself.* For example, read a book, ride your bike, or play video games for a few minutes.
² _____
_____

For instance, you can work out with people in your family, or
³ _____
_____

⁴ _____
_____
_____ In fact, most teens need eight to 10 hours of sleep.

REVIEW UNITS 1–2

1 Write two correct sentences for each picture.

> I hate storms with heavy rain.
> I hope this heat wave ends soon.
> ✓ I love blizzards.
> I'm exhausted from working in the hot weather.
> I'm stressed out from driving in bad weather.
> I'm terrified of thunder and lightning.
> It's wonderful to see all of the snow.
> The hail is awful.

1. *I love blizzards.*
   _____

2. _____
   _____

3. _____
   _____

4. _____
   _____

2 Complete the sentences with the simple present or simple past forms of the phrases.

> do something creative
> ✓ not get enough sleep
> not help around the house
> shop for clothes
> stay out late on the weekend
> work out

1. I usually *don't get enough sleep* during the week. I go to bed late and get up early.

2. I often _____. I hang out with friends Friday and Saturday nights.

3. Last week, my sister and I _____ at the mall. I spent $100.

4. Dan _____ at the gym for two hours yesterday.

5. They usually _____ when they're stressed out, like take photos.

6. Kelly _____ last weekend because she wasn't home.

3 Complete the sentences with the present continuous forms of the verbs. Then label each situation with the correct category.

> Clothes and money
> Entertainment
> ✓ Health care
> Food and drink
> Transportation
> Education

1. The doctors *are helping* (help) sick people in another country right now. *Health care*

2. Felipe _____ (study) law these days. _____

3. Shelly _____ (take) the bus right now because the train _____ (not run). _____

4. We _____ (have) sushi and tea in a Japanese restaurant right now. _____

5. Adam and Elsa _____ (watch) a comedy at the movie theater. _____

6. I _____ (not pay) for jeans and these T-shirts with cash. I _____ (use) my credit card. _____

4 Complete the paragraph with the simple past or past continuous forms of the verbs.

Last night, I ¹ _was sleeping_ (sleep) when it ² _____ (start) to rain. I ³ _____ (walk) to the window when I ⁴ _____ (hear) thunder. My parents ⁵ _____ (watch) a movie on TV when I ⁶ _____ (scream). They ⁷ _____ (run) to my room. They ⁸ _____ (wonder) what happened when they ⁹ _____ (see) that I was terrified of the thunder! After that, we ¹⁰ _____ (watch) the movie together, and then I ¹¹ _____ (go) to bed. I ¹² _____ (fall) asleep when my cat ¹³ _____ (jump) on my bed. I definitely ¹⁴ _____ (not get) enough sleep last night!

5 Circle the correct answers.

1. Julie is sick. She **had better** / **had better not** see a doctor.
2. We **must** / **must not** pay with a credit card. This restaurant only takes cash.
3. You **have to** / **don't have to** help around the house today. It's a mess!
4. Nelson and Ben **should** / **shouldn't** stay out so late. They're always exhausted in the morning.
5. We **ought to** / **ought not to** wear helmets when we ride our bikes on that road. It's dangerous.
6. You **must** / **must not** do your homework before you can hang out with friends.
7. Wendy **has to** / **doesn't have to** walk to school. She takes the bus.
8. You **had better** / **had better not** be late to class. The teacher is strict about being on time.
9. We **should** / **shouldn't** buy Tim a gift. It's his birthday tomorrow.
10. Ray **ought to** / **ought not to** drive without a license.

6 Write sentences with your own opinions. Use *It's (not)* + adjective + infinitive.

1. easy / ride / a bike

   It's easy to ride a bike. OR
   It's not easy to ride a bike.

2. fun / go / to amusement parks
   _____
3. smart / spend / money on an education
   _____
4. difficult / learn / English
   _____
5. important / have / time for yourself
   _____
6. hard / get / enough sleep
   _____
7. boring / watch TV / every weekend
   _____

7 Circle the correct answers.

1. **A:** Do you know how to fix a computer?
   B: No. _____
   a. I'm not very good at things like that.
   b. It's really pretty simple.
2. **A:** It's difficult to lift this heavy box.
   B: Wait. _____
   a. Let me show you.
   b. I'll give you a hand if you like.
3. **A:** It's hot in here. _____
   B: Yeah, but I like hot weather.
   a. I don't think so.
   b. Don't you think?
4. **A:** Our homework is confusing.
   B: I know. _____
   a. I'm not sure how to do it.
   b. I disagree.
5. **A:** I really want to beat this video game! Can you help me?
   B: Sure. _____
   a. I'm not very good at things like that.
   b. I'll give you a hand if you like.
6. **A:** Well, I'm glad we left at 6:00 like you wanted. These are great seats!
   B: _____ It's always good to go early.
   a. Don't you think?
   b. See what I mean?

3 Art All Around Us

VOCABULARY Visual arts

1. Match the clues on the left with the things and people on the right. Some items have more than one answer.

   1. a person __e__, ____
   2. done on a wall ____, ____
   3. done with a pencil ____
   4. always done on a computer ____
   5. a lot of art in one place ____
   6. art made with the hands that isn't flat ____, ____
   7. usually in a book ____

   a. digital art
   b. pottery
   c. exhibition
   d. comics
   e. living statue
   f. mural
   g. sculpture
   h. drawing
   i. portrait painter
   j. graffiti

2. What kind of art are the materials below used for? Label the pictures with some of the words from Exercise 1.

   1. ____pottery____   2. _____
   3. _____   4. _____
   5. _____   6. _____

3. Complete the sentences with some of the words from Exercise 1.

   1. A famous Diego Rivera _____ is at the Detroit Institute of Arts. It's a painting of factory workers painted on a wall in the museum.
   2. My grandmother is a _____. She paints pictures of famous people.
   3. I am a _____ in New York City. I dress up as the Statue of Liberty.
   4. There's a great _____ of modern art at the museum.

4. Answer the questions with your own information.

   1. What kind of art do you like to see at exhibitions?
      I like to see Renaissance art at exhibitions.
   2. What kind of art do you have in your home or room?
      _____
   3. Do you have an art class or did you take an art class in the past? What kind of art do/did you make?
      _____
   4. Do you like comics? Why? / Why not?
      _____

GRAMMAR Verb + -ing form (gerund) review

1. Correct the sentences. Use the simple present and the -ing form of a verb (gerund).

   1. John loves ~~go~~ *going* to museums.
   2. Isabel enjoying taking art classes.
   3. We not like watching living statues. It's boring.
   4. I don't mind to help my dad when he paints.
   5. Cal and Vera hate draw pictures.
   6. Marcia loves read comics. She reads them all the time.

2 Complete the two sentences about each picture with the correct verbs. Use the simple present and the -ing form of a verb.

✓ like   look   ✓ make   not enjoy

1. Kate ___likes making___ pottery.
   She _____ at sculptures.

hate   love   play   ride

2. Joe _____ his skateboard.
   He _____ soccer.

run   enjoy   not like   get

3. Sparky _____ in the park.
   She _____ a bath.

love   not mind   play   walk

4. Dina and Ki _____ soccer in the park. They _____ to school.

3 Put the words in order to make sentences. Change the correct verbs to the -ing form.

1. enjoy / on the weekends / Stacey / shop / for clothes
   Stacey enjoys shopping for clothes
   on the weekends.

2. camp / and Dan / in the mountains / Tyler / love
   _____
   _____

3. to / go / I / art exhibitions / don't enjoy
   _____
   _____

4. around / don't mind / the house / we / help
   _____
   _____

5. of her cat / Donna / paint / loves / portraits
   _____
   _____

6. watch / hate / horror movies / you
   _____
   _____

4 Write sentences that are true for you with the simple present and the -ing form of a verb. Use the phrases (not) like, (not) love, hate, (not) enjoy, or not mind.

1. ride a bike
   I love riding a bike.

2. go to museums
   _____

3. watch living statues
   _____

4. draw pictures
   _____

5. take photos
   _____

6. help around the house
   _____

Unit 3 | 17

VOCABULARY Musical instruments

1 Look at the pictures and complete the crossword.

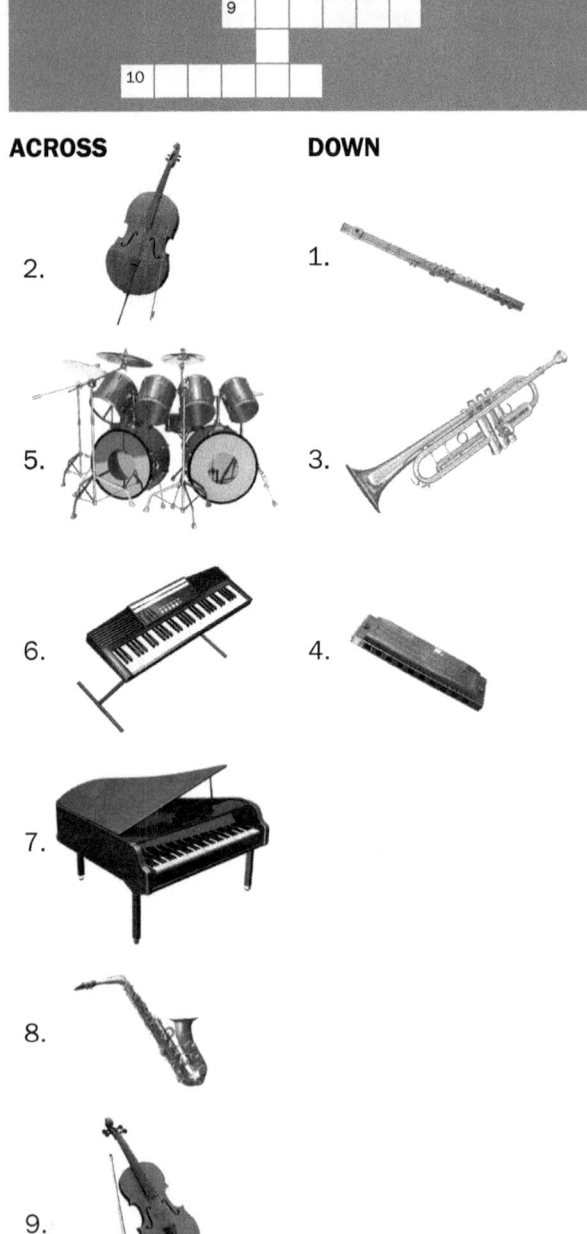

2. cello

ACROSS

2.
5.
6.
7.
8.
9.
10.

DOWN

1.
3.
4.

2 Check (✓) the items that are true for each instrument. Sometimes more than one answer is possible.

	You use your mouth to play this.	You use your hands to play this.	It has strings.
1. a trumpet	✓	✓	
2. drums			
3. a guitar			
4. a keyboard			
5. a cello			
6. a piano			
7. a flute			
8. a harmonica			
9. a violin			
10. a saxophone			

3 Look at the pictures in Exercise 1 again. Write sentences about the instruments the people are playing. Use the present continuous.

1. _Tia is playing a guitar._
2. _____
3. _____
4. _____
5. _____
6. _____

18 | Unit 3

GRAMMAR -ing forms (gerunds) as subjects

1 Write the *-ing* forms of the verbs.

1. draw *drawing*
2. take _____
3. run _____
4. make _____
5. feel _____
6. shop _____
7. care _____
8. play _____

2 Complete the sentences with the *-ing* forms of the verbs from Exercise 1.

1. *Drawing* outside is very relaxing.
2. _____ the drums loudly is fun.
3. _____ for animals is a big responsibility.
4. _____ is really good exercise.
5. _____ for clothes can take a lot of time.
6. _____ pottery is harder than it looks.
7. _____ photos is Sonya's favorite thing to do.
8. _____ exhausted is not good for you.

3 Write the activities in the order you like doing them. Use the *-ing* forms of the verbs. 1 = the activity you like the best.

chat with friends
do something creative
play a musical instrument
ride on a roller coaster
visit a museum

1. _____
2. _____
3. _____
4. _____
5. _____

Verbs + prepositions + *-ing* forms (gerunds)

4 Write sentences. Use verbs + prepositions + *-ing* forms.

1. not apologize / for / make / mistakes isn't a good idea

   Not apologizing for making mistakes isn't a good idea.

2. you need to / concentrate / on / study

   _____

3. our lessons / consist / of / make / pottery and jewelry

   _____

4. Janice / feel / like / play / her guitar right now

   _____

5. not believe / in / have / time for yourself can have negative results

   _____

6. I / decide / against / go / to the concert

   _____

5 Answer the questions with your own ideas. Use *-ing* forms as subjects or use a verb + a preposition + the *-ing* form of a verb.

1. What do you think about painting?

   Painting is hard, but some people are good at it.

2. When do you concentrate on studying?

   _____

3. What's your opinion about exercising?

   _____

4. What do you worry about?

   _____

5. What have you apologized for doing?

   _____

6. What do you think about learning to play an instrument?

   _____

Unit 3 | 19

CONVERSATION Inviting a friend and arranging to meet

1 Circle the correct words.

1. **How** / **Should** about going to the Museum of Modern Art tomorrow?
2. **How** / **What** time should we meet?
3. **Should** / **Sounds** good.
4. **What** / **Should** I ask my brother to take us?
5. **That's** / **Sounding** a good idea.

2 Complete the conversation with the phrases from Exercise 1.

Mateo: Hi, Sara. ¹ *How about going to the Museum of Modern Art tomorrow?*

Sara: Really? I thought you hated going to museums.

Mateo: Well, I usually do, but there's a really cool digital art exhibition. They have pictures of skateboarders that an artist created on a computer.

Sara: Cool! I'd like seeing that.

Mateo: OK. The museum is kind of far, but we can ride our bikes.

Sara: ² _____ He won't mind driving.

Mateo: ³ _____ I can come to your house then. ⁴ _____

Sara: Well, he doesn't like getting up early. How about 11:00 a.m.?

Mateo: ⁵ _____

20 | Unit 3

READING TO WRITE

1 Answer the questions with information from the poster.

ROCK WITH US!
DOKK is playing this Friday!
Come and hear our new songs on Friday, April 10, at 9:00 p.m. at Newtown Park.

1. What's the name of the band?
   _____
2. What kind of music do they play?
   _____
3. When are they playing?
   _____
4. Where are they playing?
   _____

2 Circle the correct words.

Gina: How ¹**was** / **were** the concert last night?

Barry: It ²**was** / **were** great! I love listening to live music.

Gina: Who played?

Barry: DOKK. The band's name ³**is** / **are** from the first letters of the members' names – Donna, Olivia, Kevin, and Kim.

Gina: Cool. Where ⁴**is** / **are** the band from?

Barry: They ⁵**is** / **are** from Austin, Texas. They write their own music. Donna ⁶**is** / **are** an amazing drummer, Kevin and Kim play the guitar, and Olivia sings. Last night, they ⁷**was** / **were** amazing! I liked the concert because they played my favorite songs, and they played their new songs, too.

Gina: ⁸**Is** / **Are** it your favorite band?

Barry: Well, no. My favorite band ⁹**is** / **are** The Three Joshes, but I like DOKK a lot. They ¹⁰**is** / **are** really popular. There ¹¹**was** / **were** a big crowd last night. I think there ¹²**was** / **were** over 500 people at the concert.

Gina: Wow! Next time they play, let me know, and I'll go with you.

3 Complete Barry's blog post about the concert. Use the information in the poster from Exercise 1 and the conversation from Exercise 2.

LAST WEEKEND'S CONCERT
Posted on April 8

I went to a great concert last weekend at ¹ _Newtown Park_ . There were ² _____ people at the concert. Most of them were teenagers. A band named ³ _____ played. They are a ⁴ _____ band from Austin, ⁵ _____ . There are ⁶ _____ people in the band. Their band name is from ⁷ _____ of their names. The concert was ⁸ _____ ! I liked it because they played my ⁹ _____ . Their ¹⁰ _____ were also really good. If they play in your city, you have to go see this band!

4 Sign Me Up!

VOCABULARY Adventure travel

1 Find eight more words associated with travel activities.

N	H	I	M	H	K	C	C	A	M	W	U	M	K	M
B	B	S	O	Z	J	R	A	F	T	I	N	G	Q	N
T	B	L	U	N	B	U	I	C	R	U	I	S	E	Z
O	A	I	N	M	D	I	Y	B	N	A	B	N	L	R
S	C	U	T	I	G	Z	I	N	G	Y	A	T	A	O
H	K	S	A	I	L	I	N	G	P	G	L	E	S	C
M	P	F	I	Y	C	B	Q	X	A	G	L	R	L	K
R	A	S	N	R	H	I	Q	U	R	B	O	M	M	C
G	C	Z	B	C	K	M	O	U	N	F	O	Y	O	L
T	K	Y	I	X	D	E	P	C	N	E	N	A	T	I
D	I	W	K	N	X	S	A	F	A	R	I	F	P	M
G	N	K	I	S	I	S	L	E	R	P	N	E	S	B
I	G	X	N	T	S	A	F	A	N	A	G	S	U	I
Y	P	Y	G	B	Q	F	N	H	B	O	G	P	F	N
T	S	U	M	M	E	R	C	A	M	P	D	I	A	G

2 Check (✓) the activities that involve water.

1. ❑ go backpacking
2. ❑ go on a cruise
3. ❑ go ballooning
4. ❑ go mountain biking
5. ❑ go on a safari
6. ❑ go rafting
7. ❑ go rock climbing
8. ❑ go sailing
9. ❑ go to summer camp

3 Complete Javier's email with some of the expressions from Exercise 2. Use the simple past.

To: Tim
From: Javier
Subject: My summer at camp

Hey Tim,

I'm so glad that I ¹ _went to summer camp_. At first, I didn't want to be away from home this summer, but I'm having a great time. There are a lot of cool activities here. Last week, we ² _____ on the lake. We took two boats so that everyone at camp could go. We also ³ _____ on the Red River. It was very fast! I ⁴ _____, too. I had to wear a helmet and use ropes to get to the top of the mountain! On Saturday, we ⁵ _____. My bag was really heavy because I brought a lot of water and food for the hike. On Sunday, we ⁶ _____ on some trails. I was glad that I brought my bike to camp, so I didn't have to rent one.

Yesterday was the best! We ⁷ _____. It was amazing! We were so high up in the sky.

I can't believe that you ⁸ _____. Did you see any elephants, lions, or giraffes? Write soon and tell me all about your trip.

Your friend,
Javier

4 Answer the questions with your own information.

1. Which activities from Exercise 2 have you done?
   I have gone rafting, and I have gone on a cruise.
   _____

2. Which activities would you like to do?
   _____

3. Which activities wouldn't you want to try?
   _____

GRAMMAR Present perfect with *already, yet,* and *just*; present perfect questions

1 Read the sentences. Circle the answer that correctly explains each situation.

1. The boat hasn't left yet.
   a. The boat left.   (**b. The boat didn't leave.**)
2. They've already left for summer camp.
   a. They are at home.   b. They aren't at home.
3. We have just seen lions on a safari.
   a. We saw lions a few minutes ago.   b. We saw lions a week ago.
4. They haven't cleaned the boat yet.
   a. They won't clean the boat.   b. They will probably clean the boat later.
5. Calvin has just told me about his trip.
   a. Calvin told me about his trip recently.   b. Calvin told me about his trip a while ago.

2 Rewrite the sentences and questions with the words in parentheses.

1. Have you left the house? (yet)
   Have you left the house yet?
2. I have told Todd our travel plans. (already)
   _____
3. Jenna has taken a picture of a monkey. (just)
   _____
4. They haven't gone rafting. (yet)
   _____
5. Has Sheila called you? (yet)
   _____

3 Put the words in order to make sentences.

1. decided / rafting / just / to go / we / have
   We have just decided to go rafting.
2. about / already / sailing / seen / that documentary / I / have
   _____
   _____
3. his / Peng / packed / yet / hasn't / bags /
   _____
   _____
4. have / already / the cruise / for / my parents / left
   _____
   _____
5. summer camp / has / from / Carolina / gotten back / just
   _____
   _____
6. about / you / your / yet / told me / trip / haven't
   _____
   _____

4 Look at the picture. Write sentences about Emma's activities. Use *already* and *yet*.

To Do
buy sunglasses
call my grandma ✓

1. pack her suitcase
   Emma has packed her suitcase already.
2. pack her tablet
   She _____
3. shut down her tablet
   _____
4. clean her room
   _____
5. buy sunglasses
   _____
6. call her grandma
   _____

VOCABULARY Phrasal verbs related to travel

1. Complete the sentences with a word or phrase from each box.

come	✓look	around	✓out
find	look	back	out
give	make	forward to	sure
look	take	off	up

1. _Look out_! That rock is going to fall.
2. We're closed. Please _____ tomorrow.
3. I want to _____ more about rock climbing in this area.
4. Don't _____. With a little practice, you'll be great at mountain biking.
5. Our plane will _____ in about an hour.
6. Please _____ you wear a helmet when you're biking.
7. Many people _____ summer vacation.
8. Let's _____ the nature center after we hike.

2 Correct the sentences.

1. I'm not looking forward ~~of~~ *to* going home.
2. Sharon has already found in about the rock climbing class.
3. You need to take sure you wear hiking boots on the trails.
4. I don't want to give out, but this is really hard.
5. Did your plane take up on time?
6. David hasn't looked back from Ecuador yet.
7. I want to go to the market and find around a little.

3 Complete the quiz questions with some of the phrasal verbs from Exercise 1. Then circle the answers that are true for you.

1. Who _makes sure_ you get up on time?
   a. I do.
   b. My parents.
   c. My brother or sister.

2. What do you _____ the most?
   a. Vacation.
   b. Weekends.
   c. Concerts.

3. When do you _____ on something?
   a. Never!
   b. When it is too hard.
   c. When it takes too much time.

4. Which of these things would you most like to _____ about?
   a. Nature trails in my area.
   b. Rock climbing adventures.
   c. Sailing classes.

5. When do you like to _____ in a store the most?
   a. When I'm buying something for myself.
   b. When I'm buying something for my family.
   c. When I'm buying something for a friend.

GRAMMAR Present perfect with *for* and *since*

1 Write the expressions in the correct places in the chart. Add *for* or *since*.

✓a week	last Tuesday	2013	a month
two days	5:00 p.m.	six hours	April

for	since
for a week	

24 | Unit 4

2 Circle the correct words.

1. Lia has been a rock climbing instructor **for** / **since** 2010.
2. Jordan's been in Jamaica **for** / **since** two weeks.
3. You haven't called me **for** / **since** three days.
4. Britt hasn't been rafting **for** / **since** July.
5. I haven't seen Marcos **for** / **since** 3:00.
6. Have you been studying **for** / **since** an hour?

3 Complete the paragraph with the present perfect forms of the verbs and *for* or *since*.

River Valley Summer Camp

Join us this summer at our wonderful camp. River Valley Summer Camp ¹ _has been open_ (be open) _since_ 2001. Hundreds of teens ² _____ (enjoy) our camp _____ over 10 years.

Meet Martin: He ³ _____ (be) a camp leader _____ 2012. He ⁴ _____ (teach) rafting classes _____ five years. This year, he will lead our new river rafting adventures.

Meet Aya: She ⁵ _____ (cook) delicious meals for our camp _____ last June. You'll love the food at River Valley.

Meet Max and Judy: They ⁶ _____ (know) each other _____ eight years. They met at River Valley eight years ago, and they got married last year. Now they run the sailing classes together.

⁷ _____ you _____ (want) to come to a summer camp _____ a long time? Sign up for River Valley today!

How long . . . ? and the present perfect

4 Look at Eric's activities. Write questions with *How long* and the present perfect. Then answer the questions.

live in Kenya	2009
work at a nature center	two years
be a safari guide	a month
teach nature classes	July
have his website about safaris	2012

1. *How long has Eric lived in Kenya?*
   He's lived in Kenya since 2009.
2. _____
3. _____
4. _____
5. _____

5 Answer the questions with your own information.

1. How long have you lived in your city?
   I've lived in my city since I was five years old.
2. How long has your family lived in your house?
   _____
3. How long have you been a student?
   _____
4. How long have you studied English?
   _____
5. How long have you and your best friend known each other?
   _____
6. How long have you owned a computer?
   _____

CONVERSATION Signing up for an adventure activity

1 **Circle the correct phrases.**

Emily: Hello. ¹**Does the price include / Can I ask you a few things about** the ballooning trip?

Guide: Sure. What would you like to know?

Emily: ²**How long is / Where can I sign up** the trip?

Guide: It's from 2:00 to 6:00, but you're only in the air for about two hours. First, we give you safety information about ballooning.

Emily: OK. ³**What about / Is it only for** adults?

Guide: No. But if you're under 18, an adult must be with you.

Emily: I see. ⁴**What do I need to bring / Where can I sign up?**

Guide: Not much. But you should wear a jacket. It can be cold up in the air. It's an amazing experience.

Emily: ⁵**How long is / What about** cameras? Can I bring mine?

Guide: Of course. You just have to be really careful with it. You don't want it to fall out of the balloon!

2 **Complete the conversation with the correct phrases.**

> ✓ Can I ask you a few things about
> Does the price include
> How long is
> Is it only for
> Where can I sign up

Noah: ¹ *Can I ask you a few things about* the rock climbing trip?

Guide: Of course.

Noah: ² _____ experienced climbers?

Guide: No, not at all. It's for beginners, too.

Noah: Great. ³ _____ equipment?

Guide: Yes, it does. We provide helmets, knee pads, and everything else you need.

Noah: OK. ⁴ _____ it?

Guide: You can choose a two-hour or four-hour adventure. It's a lot of fun, and our guides will help you with everything.

Noah: Sounds great. ⁵ _____ ?

Guide: Right here!

READING TO WRITE

1 Read the sentences that compare house parties in Ecuador and the United States. Match the sentences that are about the same topics.

Ecuador	The United States
1. People wait for the host to serve them food. _d_	a. Guests sometimes bring food to the party.
2. People usually play music and dance. ___	b. Parties can be big or small.
3. The host usually makes all of the food. ___	c. Most people dress casually.
4. Younger people often wear informal clothing, but older people often dress up. ___	d. The host often puts food on a table, and guests help themselves.
5. Parties are various sizes – from a few people to many friends. ___	e. People often listen to music while they talk.

2 Complete the sentences with the correct words.

also	either . . . or
although	however
✓ both . . . and	not only . . . but also . . .

¹ _Both_ people from South America _and_ Asia often shake hands when they greet people from the United States or Canada.

When people in Asia meet for the first time, they often give each other business cards. ² _____ people in South America don't always give each other business cards, they may exchange phone numbers and emails.

In South America, people ³ _____ kiss each other on the cheek _____ hug each other. In Asia, ⁴ _____, people do not touch each other when they say hello. They bow. ⁵ _____ do they bow when they say hello, _____ they _____ bow when they say goodbye.

3 Write the pieces of the article from Exercise 2 under the correct headings.

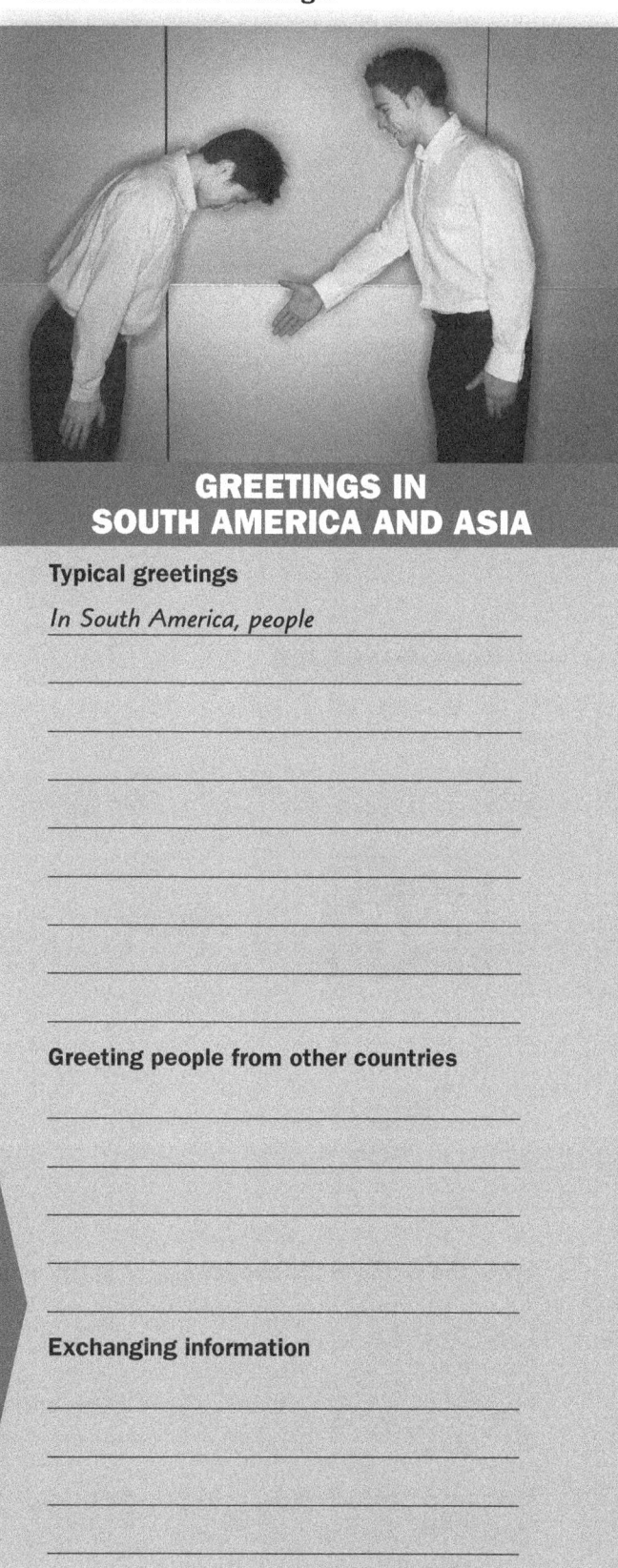

GREETINGS IN SOUTH AMERICA AND ASIA

Typical greetings

In South America, people _____
_____
_____
_____
_____
_____
_____
_____
_____

Greeting people from other countries
_____
_____
_____
_____
_____

Exchanging information
_____
_____
_____
_____
_____
_____

REVIEW UNITS 3–4

1 Look at the pictures and complete the puzzle. Find out what John did on vacation by filling in the gray boxes.

John went _____ on vacation.

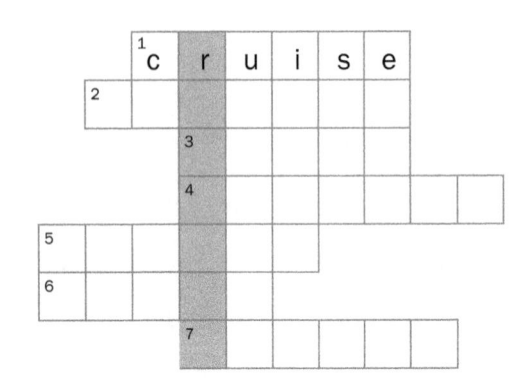

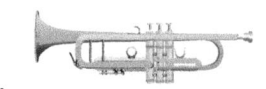

```
    1
    c  r  u  i  s  e
 2
       3
       4
 5
 6
       7
```

1.
2.
3.
4.
5.
6.
7.

2 Write the words in the correct places in the chart.

backpacking	graffiti	a safari
ballooning	a harmonica	sailing
a cello	✓ a mural	a saxophone
drums	pottery	a sculpture

Art	Music	Travel
a mural	_____	_____
_____	_____	_____
_____	_____	_____
_____	_____	_____

3 Complete the sentences with the simple present forms of the phrases. Use a verb + -ing form (gerund).

> hate / come back
> ✓ love / find out
> not enjoy / make sure
> not like / give up
> not mind / look around

1. Lauren ___*loves finding out*___ about new places.
2. Terrance _____ home after vacation.
3. I _____ when I try something new.
4. My brother _____ when I go shopping.
5. My mother _____ I've done my chores.

4 Complete the sentences with the -ing forms of the verbs. Add a preposition when necessary.

¹___*Being*___ (be) a portrait painter is an amazing job. I love it, and I think ²___*about drawing*___ (draw) all the time! I studied digital art in high school, but in college, I concentrated ³_____ (learn) to draw. ⁴_____ (not follow) my dream would have been a mistake. Now my work consists ⁵_____ (paint) portraits of interesting people. ⁶_____ (work) with new people can be difficult. They have to sit for hours, and ⁷_____ (sit) still is difficult, especially for children. My clients may get tired, but I don't worry ⁸_____ (be) bored. I love my job, and I always will!

5 Look at Alexis's To Do list. Then complete sentences about her activities. Use the present perfect with *already* and *yet*. ✓ = She's done it.

TO DO:
✓ go to the photo exhibition with Anna
practice the violin
pack clothes for summer camp
✓ buy my dad's birthday present
help around the house with Josh
✓ do my homework

1. Alexis and Anna _have already gone to the photo exhibition._
2. Alexis _____
3. She _____
4. She _____
5. Alexis and Josh _____
   _____
6. Alexis _____

6 Complete the conversation with the present perfect forms of the verbs and *already*, *yet*, or *just*.

Rick: Hey, Carla. ¹ _Have_ you _had_ dinner _yet_ ? (have / yet)

Carla: No, I ² _____. But I
³ _____ _____ lunch. (finish / just)

Rick: Oh, OK. Well, do you want to go out for dinner in a few hours?

Carla: Sounds good. ⁴ _____ you _____ at that new Mexican restaurant _____? (eat / yet)

Rick: Yes, I ⁵ _____. I
⁶ _____ _____ there three times. (be / already)

Carla: But ⁷ _____ you _____ the chicken tostadas _____? (try / yet)

Rick: No, I ⁸ _____. Let's go and I'll try them!

7 Write questions for the answers. Then complete the answers with *for* or *since*.

1. _How long has she been on a safari?_
   She's been on a safari _for_ ten days.
2. _____
   They've lived in Chicago _____ 2006.
3. _____
   I've played the saxophone _____ six months.
4. _____
   We've known Raul _____ three years.
5. _____
   He's worked at the summer camp _____ June.

8 Complete the conversations with the correct phrases.

> Does the price include
> ✓ How about going
> How long is
> Is it only for
> What do I need to bring
> What time should we meet

1. **A:** What do you want to do today?
   B: _How about going_ to the digital art exhibition at the museum?

2. **A:** _____ the backpacking trip?
   B: Five days.

3. **A:** _____?
   B: A warm jacket and hiking boots.

4. **A:** _____ transportation?
   B: Yes, it does. We take you to the river on a bus.

5. **A:** _____ beginners?
   B: No, it isn't. We have classes for advanced climbers.

6. **A:** _____?
   B: How about 6:00 p.m.?

5 Yikes!

VOCABULARY Fears

1 Circle seven more words about fears.

cthedarksnaelevatorstsngpqflyingbirectclownsvathoptdsnakesingheiinsectstgifpsmnheightsabtwlfqpbirdsflatnf

2 Look at the pictures. Complete the sentences with the correct fears from Exercise 1.

1. Tao and Sherry are afraid of ___heights___, and they're afraid of _____.

2. Vic is afraid of _____ and _____.

3. Alicia is afraid of _____ and _____.

4. Ed is afraid of _____ and _____.

3 Circle the correct words in the quiz. Then check (✓) the answers that are true for you. Add your points.

How fearful are you?

	Always true 3 points	Sometimes true 2 points	Never true 1 point
1 I take the stairs because I hate riding in **elevators** / **the dark**.			
2 I don't like hiking because **snakes** / **flying** scare me.			
3 I don't go to the circus because I'm afraid of **insects** / **clowns**.			
4 I can't walk on high bridges because I'm afraid of **heights** / **clowns**.			
5 I sleep with a nightlight because I'm afraid of **heights** / **the dark**.			
6 **Snakes** / **Birds** scare me when they fly over my head.			
7 I'm afraid of **elevators** / **flying**. I hate planes!			
8 I don't like to sit on the ground because I'm afraid of **insects** / **birds**.			

My points: _____

17–24 points: You're afraid of a lot of things. It can stop you from doing things.

9–16 points: You have some fears, but you can probably overcome them.

8 points: You aren't afraid of anything!

GRAMMAR Future review – *will, be going to*, present continuous

1 Read the sentences and check (✓) the correct columns.

	Planned event	Decided at the moment of speaking
1. Hey, I think I'll go to the store with you.		✓
2. Paul is going to study in Mexico next year.		
3. I'm not working on Saturday.		
4. I don't know the answer. Janice will tell you.		
5. Sean is taking a test in an hour.		
6. I'm not going to go on the camping trip because I'm afraid of insects.		
7. No, I won't hike to the top of the mountain. I'm afraid of heights.		
8. Sakura is going to take a class about facing fears.		

2 Rewrite the sentences. Change the present continuous to *be going to* and use the words in parentheses.

1. Sandra is shopping with Rachel tomorrow. (next week)

   Sandra is going to shop with Rachel
   next week.

2. My brother is getting married in two days. (next year)

   _____

3. We are going to Rio de Janeiro next week. (in April)

   _____

4. I'm talking to the teacher in a few minutes. (after class)

   _____

5. Pam is going on a safari on Monday. (next month)

   _____

6. They're watching a movie tonight. (on Saturday)

   _____

3 Complete the conversations with the correct forms of *will* and the words in parentheses.

1. **A:** What are you going to do tomorrow?
   B: I don't know. Maybe _____*I'll go*_____ (I / go) to the mall.

2. **A:** Do you and Don want to go to dinner with me after class?
   B: Sure. _____ (we / eat) with you.

3. **A:** Can I borrow your tablet?
   B: Sorry, I need it. But _____ (I / give) it to you when I'm done.

4. **A:** Where are you going on vacation?
   B: I'm not sure, but _____ (we / not choose) somewhere cold.

5. **A:** Do you want to take the elevator?
   B: No! I hate elevators. _____ (I / take) the stairs.

First conditional

4 Complete the paragraph with the first conditional.

Rita is afraid of snakes. If she
¹ ____*sees*____ (see) a snake, she
² _____ (not move).
If the snake ³ _____ (move), she
⁴ _____ (scream). If she
⁵ _____ (scream), her brother
⁶ _____ (hear) her. If Rita's
brother ⁷ _____ (see) her with
the snake, he ⁸ _____ (not help).
If he ⁹ _____ (laugh), Rita
¹⁰ _____ (cry). I hope Rita
doesn't see a snake!

VOCABULARY -ed and -ing adjective endings

1 Complete the chart.

	-ed	-ing
1.	embarrassed	embarrassing
2.		confusing
3.	interested	
4.		surprising
5.	exhausted	
6.		terrifying
7.	disgusted	
8.		relaxing

2 Complete the sentences with some of the words from Exercise 1. Then check (✓) if the sentences are true for you.

	Yes	No
1. I think space is _interesting_. There's always something new to learn about.		
2. I always feel _____ at the beach. The sound of the ocean makes me feel calm.		
3. Exercising is _____. I'm always tired after I work out.		
4. Yuck! I think snakes are _____.		
5. I was _____ on my last birthday! My parents had a party for me and invited all of my friends.		
6. I was _____ about my last test scores. I didn't do very well.		
7. I think clowns are _____. They really scare me.		
8. I'm never _____ in class. I always understand everything!		

3 Complete the sentences with the -ed or -ing adjective of the words in parentheses.

1. Martina is __disgusted__ (disgust) by insects.
2. Henry was _____ (exhaust) after he walked up eight flights of stairs.
3. Lori thinks her parents are _____ (embarrass) when they yell at her soccer games.
4. My little sister is _____ (terrify) of sleeping in the dark.
5. It was _____ (surprise) to find out Tara moved to Los Angeles.
6. Our homework assignment was _____ (confuse). No one understood the directions.
7. I'm not very _____ (interest) in science, but I love math.
8. Some people are afraid of flying, but I think it's _____ (relax).

GRAMMAR Modals of probability: *must, can't, may, might, could*

1 Read the sentences and check (✓) the correct columns.

	Almost certain	Impossible	Possible
1. Ramon must be from Mexico.	✓		
2. I might not have homework this weekend.			
3. We may not work tomorrow.			
4. Hillary can't be 16.			
5. My cousin could be at the mall.			
6. You must be exhausted.			

2 Match the sentences.

1. Laura wasn't in class today. _c_	a. She may not be hungry.
2. Kelly won't ride on roller coasters. ____	b. She could be busy.
3. Laila doesn't speak Japanese. ____	c. She might be sick.
4. Beth didn't order anything to eat. ____	d. She must be terrified of heights.
5. Nancy just ran 5 kilometers. ____	e. She can't be from Japan.
6. Mari didn't answer her phone. ____	f. She must be exhausted.

3 Complete the conversation with *must*, *can't*, or *might*.

Julia: Do you know where Kayla is?

Mike: No, I don't. She ___might___ be sick.

Julia: No, she ² _____ be sick. I talked to her this morning. She said she was coming to the party.

Mike: Hmm. How is she getting here?

Julia: She's taking the bus and then walking.

Mike: The bus ³ _____ be late. It's usually on time, but you never know!

Julia: That ⁴ _____ be true. She was already on the bus when I talked to her.

Mike: I see. Well, she ⁵ _____ have to stop at the store on her way.

Julia: Oh, yeah! That ⁶ _____ be it! She said she hadn't gotten a birthday card for Jacob yet.

Mike: Ah. Hey, do you think Jacob will be surprised?

Julia: I'm not sure. He ⁷ _____ know about the party.

Mike: Really?

Julia: Yeah. His brother ⁸ _____ keep a secret!

4 Write sentences with *must*, *can't*, or *may*.

1. Jenna / be / cold

   Jenna must be cold.

2. Isaac / go / rafting / or / go / ballooning

   _____

3. Jin-hee / be / finished with her book

   _____

4. You / be / exhausted

   _____

5. Nicole / fall off / her bike

   _____

5 Rewrite the sentences. Add the words in parentheses.

1. Paul is surprised. (might)

   Paul might be surprised.

2. It's 3:00. (must)

   _____

3. Cindy knows Julia. (could)

   _____

4. That roller coaster is terrifying. (must)

   _____

5. We expect to win the race. (can't)

   _____

6. You have the flu. (could)

   _____

CONVERSATION Expressing disbelief

1 Complete the phrases in the conversation.

Raul: Hi, Sofia. My friends and I are hiking up Cotopaxi this weekend.

Sofia: ¹N_o_ w_a_ _y_! That's cool.

Raul: Do you want to come?

Sofia: Sure. I'd love to! Can I invite Carolina?

Raul: Well, I don't know if she'd want to come. Cotopaxi is snowy once you get up high.

Sofia: So?

Raul: Well, Carolina is afraid of snow.

Sofia: ²T__ __ __'s im__ __ __ __ __ __ __ __! No one is afraid of snow.

Raul: It's true. There's even a name for it – chinophobia.

Sofia: Chinophobia? ³A__ __ y__ __ s __ __ __ __ __ __?

Raul: Yes, I am. It's a real thing, and Carolina has it.

Sofia: ⁴I d__ __'t b__ __ __ __ __ __ __ i__!

Raul: It's true. We were looking at this picture of snow one time, and she got really nervous.

Sofia: ⁵C__ __ __ o__! She got nervous just looking at snow?

Raul: Yes, she did!

Sofia: I'm going to call and ask her about it!

2 Circle the correct answers.

1. **A:** I climbed Cotopaxi in an hour.
   B: No **possible** / **(way)**! It takes expert climbers several hours.

2. **A:** Marcia is living in Quito for a year.
   B: Are you **serious** / **believing**? That's great.

3. **A:** Jorge took 10 bottles of water on the hike.
   B: **Believe** / **Come** on. His bag would have been too heavy.

4. **A:** Yolanda moved from the mountains to downtown Quito.
   B: I don't **impossible** / **believe** you. She hates busy cities.

5. **A:** There wasn't any snow on the top of Cotopaxi when we climbed it.
   B: That's **possible** / **impossible**. There's always snow on Cotopaxi.

34 | Unit 5

READING TO WRITE

1 Circle the correct expressions.

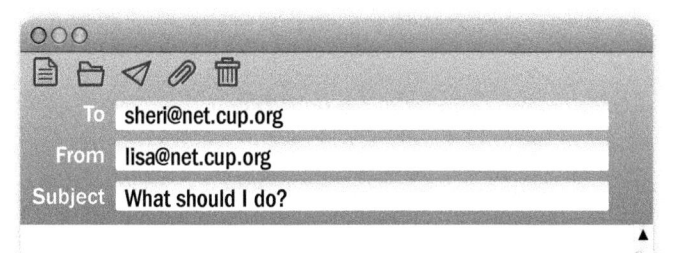

To: sheri@net.cup.org
From: lisa@net.cup.org
Subject: What should I do?

Hello Sheri,

Thanks for writing. Your summer plans sound fun. ¹**Check this out / The fact**: I'm going to go to summer camp this year. It's in the mountains, and it's going to be really fun. The ²**problem / idea** is that we live for a month without any modern technology – no cell phones, no tablets, no lights! Cool, right? ³**The problem is that / Listen to** I promised to text my little sister every day. I haven't told her that I can't yet. I'm a little nervous to tell her because I know she's going to be upset. The ⁴**idea / truth** is that I'm looking forward to not using my phone, but I just don't know what to say to my sister. What do you think I should do?

Your friend,

Lisa

2 Match the categories with the sentences from Lisa's email.

1. _d_ Greeting	a.	I haven't told her that I can't yet.
2. ___ Personal news	b.	What do you think I should do?
3. ___ The problem	c.	I promised to text my little sister every day.
4. ___ How you feel about the problem and why	d.	Hello Sheri,
5. ___ What you have/ haven't done about the problem	e.	I'm going to summer camp.
6. ___ A question to ask what your friend thinks	f.	I'm a little nervous to tell her because I know she's going to be upset.

3 Write the email in the correct order.

Because of this, I don't think I can go to the festival.

Kevin

I'm really embarrassed, and I haven't told him yet.

Your friend,

The problem is that I have acousticophobia – I'm afraid of loud noises.

What do you think I should say to him?

✓ Hi Victor,

Check this out: My cousin's band is going to play in a music festival next month.

To: victor@net.cup.org
From: kevin@net.cup.org
Subject: A problem

Hi Victor,

_____
_____
_____
_____
_____
_____
_____
_____
_____
_____
_____

Unit 5 | 35

The LONG WINTER

Unit 1 Video 1.1

BEFORE YOU WATCH

1 Look at the pictures from the video. Do you think the sentences are true (*T*) or false (*F*)?

1. These people live in a big city. _____
2. They spend most of their time outdoors. _____
3. They grow their own vegetables. _____
4. They fish in the winter. _____

WHILE YOU WATCH

2 Watch the video. Circle the correct words.

1. In Alaska, it is cold for **three / eight** months of the year.
2. The Kilcher family uses **wood / oil** to heat their home.
3. They put their **food / clothes** in storage.
4. In the winter, they **can / can't** go to a supermarket for food.
5. Atz takes traps for **rabbits / bears** into the forest.

3 Watch the video again. Complete the sentences with the correct words.

| builds | catch | cut down | goes | plan |

1. The Kilchers _____ trees in the summer.
2. They _____ fish in the lake.
3. They _____ their meals for the months ahead.
4. Atz _____ a fire on the lake.
5. He _____ home with a bag of rabbits.

AFTER YOU WATCH

4 Work with a partner. Discuss: Which do you prefer, cold weather or hot weather? What do you like to do outdoors in cold weather? In hot weather?

> I prefer cold weather. I like skiing and ice skating in cold weather. I love swimming in hot weather.

An ISLAND FLOOD

Unit 1 Video 1.3

BEFORE YOU WATCH

1 Look at the pictures from the video. Then match the pictures to the sentences.

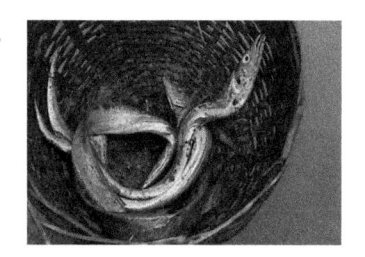

a.   b.   c.

1. These are rice fields on the island of Bali in India. _____
2. People here eat a lot of fish. _____
3. These men are fishermen – they catch fish in the sea. _____

WHILE YOU WATCH

2 Watch the video. Circle the correct words.

1. Life isn't **nice / easy** here.
2. People depend on a few **fish / rice** fields.
3. Years ago, a **flood / storm** destroyed homes.
4. The men knew they needed to **buy / build** a wall.
5. They worked for **three / five** hours.

3 Watch the video again. Match the phrases to make true sentences.

1. At last, _____   a. water flooded the village.
2. During the night, _____ b. he went fishing.
3. Last week, _____   c. the men went home.
4. Years ago, _____   d. the men watched the waters rising.

AFTER YOU WATCH

4 Work with a partner. Describe an extreme weather event in your life. What were you doing when it happened?

> Last summer, there was a big storm. There was thunder and lightning and a lot of rain. I was playing soccer. We ran into the school and closed all the windows.

Get UP and GO!

Unit 2 Video 2.1

BEFORE YOU WATCH

1 Look at the pictures from the video. Circle the correct words.

1. This special bed can wake you **up / down** in the morning.
2. It can also pull **off / in** your pajamas.
3. They purée the cereal **in / on** a blender for breakfast.

WHILE YOU WATCH

2 Watch the video. Check (✓) what the machine can do.

1. ❑ wake you
2. ❑ undress you
3. ❑ make breakfast
4. ❑ shower you
5. ❑ brush your hair

3 Watch the video again. Circle the correct answers.

1. A lot of people say they hate _____.
   a. going to bed   b. waking up   c. getting dressed
2. The machine _____ to wake you up.
   a. shakes you   b. plays music   c. showers you
3. First, they try giving the man some _____.
   a. milk   b. water   c. oatmeal
4. The man _____ the breakfast cereal.
   a. likes   b. loves   c. hates
5. What does the machine give the man at the end?
   a. shoes and socks   b. T-shirt and shorts   c. coat and hat

AFTER YOU WATCH

4 Work with a partner. Describe the differences between your morning routine during the week and on weekends. What do you do, and when?

> During the week, I get up at 6:30. I take a shower and brush my teeth. Then I get dressed. I eat breakfast around 7:00. On weekends, I usually sleep until 9. I wash my face, and then I eat breakfast. Then I get dressed around 10.

Irish DANCING

Unit 2 Video 2.3

BEFORE YOU WATCH

1 Look at the pictures from the video. Do you think the sentences are true (*T*) or false (*F*)?

In Irish dancing, you have to:

1. wear sneakers   _____
2. kick your legs high _____
3. hold your hands in the air _____
4. wear socks   _____

WHILE YOU WATCH

2 Watch the video. Circle the correct answers.

1. What does the teacher say to the dancers?
   a. Hurry up!   b. Get up!   c. Pick it up!
2. This is Julia's _____ time at the World Championship.
   a. first   b. third   c. fourth
3. Julia won the World Championship _____ years ago.
   a. one   b. two   c. three
4. This year the Championship is in _____.
   a. Belfast   b. London   c. New York City
5. Julia wins _____ place.
   a. first   b. third   c. fourth

3 Watch the video again. Number the sentences 1–5 in the order that you hear them.

1. We're on the plane right now.   _____
2. She dances tall and straight.   _____
3. I am twelve years old.   _____
4. Come on! Push it!   _____
5. I'm Julia's mom.   _____

AFTER YOU WATCH

4 Work with a partner. Do you or your classmates participate in any competitions? How do you prepare for them?

> I'm on the soccer team. We have a game every Saturday. We have to practice three times a week. We have to go to bed early the night before the game and eat a good breakfast in the morning!

Original ART

Unit 3 Video 3.1

BEFORE YOU WATCH

1 Look at the pictures from the video. Complete the sentences with the correct words.

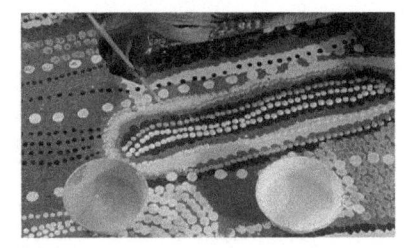

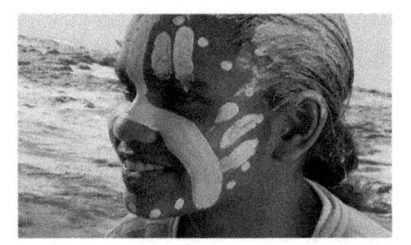

| changed | face | painting |

The Aborigines of Australia have an ancient tradition of _____. Their art is full of symbols and patterns that have not _____ in thousands of years. The dots on this girl's _____ represent rainfall.

WHILE YOU WATCH

2 Watch the video. Are the sentences true (*T*) or false (*F*)? Correct the false sentences.

1. The Aborigines have lived in Australia for 4,000 years. _____
2. The land is very important to the Aborigines. _____
3. Some paintings show where stores are. _____
4. Many symbols in their art have changed. _____
5. Aboriginal body paintings use symbols, too. _____

3 Watch the video again. Check (✔) the sentences you hear.

1. ❏ Australia is an interesting place.
2. ❏ These paintings communicate essential information about the people.
3. ❏ Our whole land is ancient.
4. ❏ Some of these paintings are survival maps.
5. ❏ Everything tells a story.

AFTER YOU WATCH

4 Work with a partner. Make a list of the symbols you see every day. What do they communicate?

I see the recycling symbol on the bins at school. It means you can put your papers there instead of in the garbage.

A WORLD of MUSIC

Unit 3 Video 3.3

BEFORE YOU WATCH

1 Look at the pictures from the video. Then match the pictures to the sentences.

a.    b.    c.

1. Indian music uses the **tabla**, a kind of drum, and the **sitar**, a stringed instrument. ____
2. An Aborigine in Australia plays the **didgeridoo**. ____
3. **Trumpets** are an important part of the Mexican mariachi sound. ____

WHILE YOU WATCH

2 Watch the video. Circle the correct answers.

1. Mariachi music has been around for ____ of years.
   a. hundreds   b. thousands   c. millions
2. The Spanish brought instruments like ____ to Mexico.
   a. sitars   b. tablas   c. guitars
3. The sitar is an ____ instrument.
   a. expensive   b. ancient   c. English
4. British musicians became interested in Indian music in the ____.
   a. 1950s   b. 1960s   c. 1970s
5. The didgeridoo is a ____ instrument.
   a. wood   b. stringed   c. wind
6. Aborigines have played didgeridoos for at least ____ years.
   a. 200   b. 2,000   c. 2,200

3 Watch the video again. Match the nouns and adjectives.

1. ____ mariachi music   a. strange
2. ____ the sitar and tabla   b. famous
3. ____ kangaroo and koala   c. lively
4. ____ didgeridoo   d. unusual

AFTER YOU WATCH

4 Work in small groups. Discuss musicians from other countries: Who do you like? Describe their music.

> I really like Lorde. She's from New Zealand. Her music is part pop, rock, and hip hop.

The AGE of DISCOVERY

Unit 4 Video 4.1

BEFORE YOU WATCH

1 Look at the picture from the video. Complete the sentences with the correct words.

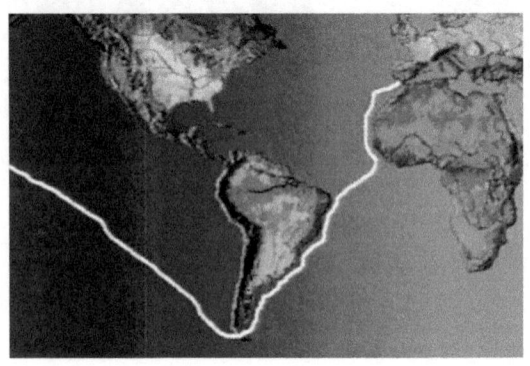

| Atlantic | Pacific | South | Spain |

In 1519, the famous explorer Ferdinand Magellan sailed from _____ across the _____ Ocean. He went around the bottom of _____ America, then crossed the _____ Ocean.

WHILE YOU WATCH

2 Watch the video. Number the events 1–5 in the order they occurred.

1. Magellan sails around South America. _____
2. One of Magellan's ships completes the journey. _____
3. Christopher Columbus discovers the Americas. _____
4. Magellan lives in a castle with the king and queen of Portugal. _____
5. Vasco de Gama sails around Africa to India. _____

3 Watch the video again. Complete the sentences with the correct places.

| Asia | Philippines | Portugal | Strait of Magellan | Spain |

1. Magellan was born in 1480 in _____.
2. Christopher Columbus was looking for _____ in 1492.
3. The king of _____ gave Magellan five boats.
4. The ocean waters in the _____ were very dangerous.
5. Magellan was killed in the _____.

AFTER YOU WATCH

4 Work in small groups. Take turns naming exciting activities you have done and activities you want to do.

> I've gone rafting. I really want to go scuba diving.

78 | Unit 4

Fun in AUSTRALIA

Unit 4 Video 4.3

BEFORE YOU WATCH

1 Look at the pictures from the video. Complete the sentences with the correct words.

camels   sheep   toads

Australia has many different kinds of animals and some very unusual sports. _____ are not easy to ride, but Australians race them. They also have contests to see who can cut a _____'s wool the fastest. In some parts of the country, people paint numbers on these small _____ and race them!

WHILE YOU WATCH

2 Watch the video. Complete the sentences with the correct words.

1. Uluru is a giant _____.
2. Australia has nearly a million wild _____.
3. The cane _____ is poisonous.
4. _____ shearing is a big sport in Australia.
5. Australian rules _____ is the country's favorite sport.

3 Watch the video again. Number the things 1–5 in the order you see them.

1. kangaroos   ____
2. sheep   ____
3. Sydney Opera House ____
4. camels   ____
5. toads   ____

AFTER YOU WATCH

4 Work with a partner. What are some other contests with animals in the world? Make a list, then share it with another pair.

Country	Animal	Contest
Ireland, Scotland, England	dogs	sheep herding

Unit 4 | 79

Creepy CREATURES

Unit 5 Video 5.1

BEFORE YOU WATCH

1 Look at the picture from the video and read the sentences. Match the words and the definitions.

1. _____ capture
2. _____ phobia
3. _____ serpent

a. snake
b. catch
c. extreme fear

4. Do you have any phobias? Explain.
_____
_____
_____

This man is <u>capturing</u> a King Cobra. Many people have a <u>phobia</u> of this <u>serpent</u>.

WHILE YOU WATCH

2 Watch the video. Are the sentences true (*T*) or false (*F*)? Correct the false sentences.

1. The video shows more than eight different kinds of snakes. _____
2. The snake around Jeff Corwin's arm scares him. _____
3. Some King Cobras live near rivers. _____
4. Jeff's friend has never seen a King Cobra before. _____
5. To catch a King Cobra, you must hold its head. _____

3 Watch the video again. Check (✓) the words you hear to describe the King Cobra.

1. ❏ nervous
2. ❏ king of the serpents
3. ❏ snake-eater
4. ❏ terrified
5. ❏ awesome

AFTER YOU WATCH

4 Work in small groups. Make a list of three to four animals that terrify people. Why do you think people are afraid of these animals? Share your list with other groups.

> 1. lions: They can attack people.
> 2. snakes: A snake bite can be poisonous.
> 3. sharks: A shark might attack you when you're swimming in the ocean.

80 | Unit 5

Calendars of the ANCIENT MAYA

Unit 5 Video 5.3

BEFORE YOU WATCH

1 Look at the pictures from the video. Circle the correct answers.

This calendar **use / was used** by the ancient Mayan civilization in Mexico and Central America. Each day **had / has had** a name and a symbol. The Maya **predicted / have predicted** good days and bad days.

2 Look at the Cimi symbol in the Mayan calendar. What do you think it means?

_____
_____
_____

WHILE YOU WATCH

3 Watch the video. Circle the correct answers.

 1. The Mayan calendar showed each **day / week** of the year.
 2. The Maya planted on **sunny / good** days.
 3. The solar calendar had **18 / 20** months.
 4. There were **five / six** bad days in a year.
 5. The temple of Kukulkan has **360 / 365** steps.

4 Watch the video again. Match the phrases to make true sentences.

 1. The Maya _____   a. had a symbol.
 2. Each day _____   b. was a good day.
 3. Imix _____   c. watched the sun and moon.
 4. Cimi _____   d. happened on bad days.
 5. Nothing important _____   e. was a bad day.

AFTER YOU WATCH

5 Work with a partner. Make a calendar for the next week. Use symbols to indicate good days and bad days. Say one good thing that will happen to your partner on the good days, and one bad thing that will happen on the bad days.

> Next Monday will be a bad day. You will lose your backpack. Next Tuesday will be a good day. You will win tickets to a concert.

This page intentionally left blank.

Irregular verbs

Base Verb	Simple Past	Past Participle
babysit	babysat	babysat
be	was, were	been
become	became	become
begin	began	begun
bleed	bled	bled
blow	blew	blown
break	broke	broken
bring	brought	brought
build	built	built
burn	burned/burnt	burned/burnt
buy	bought	bought
catch	caught	caught
choose	chose	chosen
come	came	come
cost	cost	cost
cut	cut	cut
deal	dealt	dealt
dive	dived/dove	dived
do	did	done
draw	drew	drawn
dream	dreamed/dreamt	dreamed/dreamt
drink	drank	drunk
drive	drove	driven
eat	ate	eaten
fall	fell	fallen
feel	felt	felt
fight	fought	fought
find	found	found
fly	flew	flown
forget	forgot	forgotten
freeze	froze	frozen
get	got	gotten
give	gave	given
go	went	gone
grow	grew	grown
hang	hung	hung
have	had	had
hear	heard	heard
hide	hid	hidden
hit	hit	hit
hold	held	held
hurt	hurt	hurt
keep	kept	kept

Base Verb	Simple Past	Past Participle
know	knew	known
leave	left	left
let	let	let
lie	lay	lain
lose	lost	lost
make	made	made
mean	meant	meant
meet	met	met
pay	paid	paid
put	put	put
read	read	read
ride	rode	ridden
ring	rang	rung
rise	rose	risen
run	ran	run
say	said	said
see	saw	seen
sell	sold	sold
send	sent	sent
set	set	set
show	showed	shown
shut	shut	shut
sing	sang	sung
sit	sat	sat
sleep	slept	slept
speak	spoke	spoken
spend	spent	spent
spread	spread	spread
stand	stood	stood
steal	stole	stolen
stick	stuck	stuck
swim	swam	swum
take	took	taken
teach	taught	taught
tell	told	told
think	thought	thought
throw	threw	thrown
understand	understood	understood
wake	woke	woken
wear	wore	worn
win	won	won
write	wrote	written

Credits

The authors and publishers acknowledge the following sources of copyright material and are grateful for the permissions granted. While every effort has been made, it has not always been possible to identify the sources of all the material used, or to trace all copyright holders. If any omissions are brought to our notice, we will be happy to include the appropriate acknowledgements on reprinting.

p. 2-3 (B/G): Shutterstock Images/John McCormick; p. 3 (a): Alamy/©Piero Cruciatti; p. 3 (b): Shutterstock Images/egd; p. 3 (c): Shutterstock Images/James BO Insogna; p. 3 (d): Alamy/©Matthew Chattle; p. 3 (e): Alamy/©blickwinkel; p. 3 (f): Shutterstock Images/Igumnova Irina; p. 3 (g): Getty Images/Sam Yeh/AFP; p. 4 (B/G): Shutterstock Images/Kathriba; p. 4 (TL): Getty Images/National Geographic; p. 4 (TR): Alamy/©RIA Novosti; p. 5 (CL): Alamy/©Jeff Schultz/Alaska Stock; p. 6 (B/G): Shutterstock Images/Yulia Glam; p. 7 (CR): Shutterstock Images/Andrey_Popov; p. 8 (L): Alamy/©Roy Johnson; p. 9 (TR): Shutterstock Images/Raymona Pooler; p. 10 (TL): Alamy/©Chris Howarth/South Atlantic; p. 10 (B/G): Shutterstock Images/Freesoulproduction; p. 11 (1): Shutterstock Images/Ashraf Jandali; p.11 (2): Shutterstock Images/Rarach; p.11 (3): Alamy/©Barry Diomede; p. 11 (4): Shutterstock Images/OHishiapply; p. 11 (5): Alamy/©EB Images/Blend Images; p. 11 (6): Alamy/©Paul Maguire; p. 12-13 (B/G): Corbis/JGI/Jamie Grill; p. 13 (a): Shutterstock Images/Syda Productions; p. 13 (b): Alamy/©Tetra Images; p. 13 (c): Alamy/©Kuttig – People; p. 13 (e): Shutterstock Images/Pressmaster; p.13 (g): Alamy/©Juice Images; p. 13 (f): Shutterstock Images/Masson; p. 13 (g): Superstock/age footstock; p. 13 (h): Getty Images/Image Source; p. 13 (i): Shutterstock Images/kuznetcov_konstantin; p. 14 (TL): Shutterstock Images/Lasse Kristensen; p. 15 (TR): Alamy/©PCN Photography; p. 16 (TR): Shutterstock Images/Lucky Business; p. 16 (a): Shutterstock Images/Ruslan Guzov; p. 16 (b): Shutterstock Images/Dragon Images;p. 16 (c): Shutterstock Images/Pressmaster; p. 16 (d): Shutterstock Images/Creatista; p. 16 (e): Shutterstock Images/Photographee.eu;p. 16 (f): Getty Images/Nick Dolding; p. 16 (g): Alamy/©Bjorn Andren/Robert Matton AB; p. 17 (TR): Shutterstock Images/Alexander Raths; p. 18 (TL): Alamy/©Kumar Sriskandan; p. 18 (BL): Corbis/Hill Street Studios/Blend Images; p. 19 (TR): Alamy/©Sverre Haugland; p. 20 (B/G): Shutterstock Images/William Perugini; p. 20 (T): Alamy/©AJSH Photograph; p. 21 (BR): Shutterstock Images/Andreasnikolas; p. 22-23 (B/G): Alamy/©JL Images; p. 23 (a): Alamy/©Jeff Gilbert; p. 23 (b): Alamy/©Michele and Tom Grimm;p. 23 (c):Alamy/©Arco Images GmbH; p. 23 (d): Alamy/©Paul Lovichi Photography; p. 23 (e): Alamy/©eddie linssen; p. 23 (f): Alamy/©Nagelestock.com; p. 23 (g): Alamy/©Tony French; p. 23 (h): Alamy/©Andrew Aitchison; p. 23 (i): Shutterestock/Grynold; p. 23 (j): Alamy/©Christina K; p. 24 (B/G): Shutterstock Images/Jag_cz; p. 24 (T): Alamy/©Kevin Britland; p. 25 (BL): Alamy/©LWA/Dann Tardif/Blend Images; p. 26 (TL): Alamy/©i stage; p. 26 (a): Alamy/©Aki; p. 26 (b): Shutterstock Images/Furtseff; p. 26 (c): Shutterstock Images/Vereshchagin Dmitry; p. 26 (d): Shutterstock Images/Christian Bertrand; p. 26 (e): Shutterstock Images/mphot; p. 26 (f): Shutterstock Images/Dario Sabljak; p. 26 (g): Shutterstock Images/Chromakey; p. 26 (h): Alamy/©lem; p. 26 (i):Shutterstock Images/vvoe; p. 26 (j): Shutterstock Images/ Visun Khankasem; p. 27 (TR): Alamy/©Graham Salter/Lebrecht Music & Arts; p. 28 (L): Shutterstock Images/Warren Goldswain; p. 29 (TL): Alamy/©david pearson; p. 30 (TR): Alamy/©ZUMA Press, Inc.; p. 30 (B/G): Shutterstock Images/Fluke samed; p. 32-33 (B/G): Getty Images/Vetta/Scott Hailstone; p. 33 (a): Alamy/©J.R.Bale; p. 33 (b): Superstock/age footstock; p. 33 (c): Getty Images/Ken Chernus/Taxi; p. 33 (d): Shutterstock Images/Greg Epperson; p. 33 (e): Alamy/©PhotoEdit; p. 33 (f): Alamy/©Age Fotostock Spain S.L.; p. 33 (g): Alamy/©Dmitry Burlakov; p. 33 (h): Shutterstock Images/PhotoSky; p. 33 (i): Alamy/©ZUMA Press, Inc.; p. 34 (TL): Alamy/©Gaspar Avila; p. 34 (BL): Alamy/©ZUMA Press, Inc.; p. 35 (CR): Getty Images/Tetra Images; p. 36 (TL): Getty Images/Philip and Karen Smith; p. 36 (BL): Alamy/©Westend61 GmbH; p. 37 (TR): Alamy/©Cultura; p. 38 (TL): Alamy/©Hemis; p. 38 (CL): Shutterstock Images/Strahil Dimitrov; p. 38 (BL): Shutterstock Images/Graphichead; p. 39 (TR): Corbis/Radius Images; p. 40 (T): Shutterstock Images/Pichugin Dmitry; p. 40 (a): Shutterstock Images/Bildagentur Zoonar GmbH; p. 40 (b): Alamy/©Howard Davies; p. 40 (c): Robert Harding Picture Library/Stuart Black/AgeFotostock; p. 40 (d): Alamy/©John Elk III; p. 40 (e): Shutterstock Images/Konrad Mostert; p. 40 (f): Shutterstock Images/Sasapee; p. 42-43 (B/G): Corbis/2/Andrew Bret Wallis/Ocean; p. 43 (a): Shutterstock Images/Dmitrijs Bindemanis; p. 43 (b): Shutterstock Images/Matteo photos; p. 43 (c): Alamy/©Robin Beckham/BEEPstock; p. 43 (d): Shutterstock Images/Jayakumar; p. 43 (e): Shutterstock Images/Jag_cz; p. 43 (f): Shutterstock Images/Lisa F. Young; p. 43 (g): Alamy/©Phil Degginger; p. 43 (h): Shutterstock Images/Blend Images; p. 44 (TR): Shutterstock Images/Andresr; p. 44 (1): UNIVERSAL/THE KOBAL COLLECTION/BOLAND, JASIN; p. 44 (2): UNIVERSAL/THE KOBAL COLLECTION/MOSELEY, MELISSA; p. 44 (3): HAMMER FILM PRODUCTIONS/THE KOBAL COLLECTION; p. 44 (4): MIRAMAX/THE KOBAL COLLECTION; p. 44 (5): 20TH CENTURY FOX/THE KOBAL COLLECTION/FOREMAN, RICHARD; p. 44 (6): CODE RED PRODUCTIONS/THE KOBAL COLLECTION; p. 44 (7): NEW REGENCY PICTURES/THE KOBAL COLLECTION; p. 46 (TL): Alamy/©Gunter Marx; p. 46 (BL): Alamy/©Ruby; p. 46 (BL): Alamy/©GeoStills; p. 47 (TR): Alamy/©Gunter Marx; p. 48 (B/G): Shutterstock Images/Kamira; p. 49 (TR): Shutterstock Images/Pincasso; p. 50 (TR): Alamy/©Adrian Turner; p. 50 (B/G): Shutterstock Images/Shchipkova Elena; p. 51 (TR): Shutterstock Images/Jacek Chabraszewski; p. 52-53 (B/G): Corbis/Herbert Meyrl/Westend61; p. 54-55 (B/G): Getty Images/Kevin Spreekmeester; p. 56 (TC): Shutterstock Images/Feng Yu; p. 57 (B): Alamy/©Agencja Fotograficzna Caro; p. 58 (CL): Alamy/©Denise Hager Catchlight Visual Services; p. 58 (TL): Shutterstock Images/Sean Locke Photography; p. 59 (CR): Alamy/©Richard G. Bingham II; p. 60 (TL): Shutterstock Images/IPranoffee; p. 60 (BL): Getty Images/Chris Schmidt; p. 60 (BC): Alamy/©Tony Cordoza; p. 60 (BR): Alamy/©Marjorie Kamys Cotera/Bob Daemmrich Photography; p. 61 (TL): Shutterstock Images/Ermolaev Alexander; p. 62 (B/G): Shutterstock Images/Albund; p. 62 (TL): Alamy/©Picture Partners; p. 62 (TL): Alamy/©Denise Hager Catchlight Visual Services; p. 63 (TR): Shutterstock Images/Dmitry Kalinovsky; p. 64-65 (B/G): Shutterstock Images/Albachiaraa; p. 65 (a): Shutterstock Images/Lanych; p. 65 (b): Shutterstock Images/Luchi_a; p. 65 (c): Shutterstock Images/K.Miri Photography; p. 65 (d): Shutterstock Images/Coprid; p. 65 (e): Shutterstock Images/Stockphoto Graf; p. 65 (f): Shutterstock Images/FreeBirdPhotos; p. 65 (g): Shutterstock Images/DigitalMagus; p. 65 (h): Shutterstock Images/Praisaeng; p. 65 (i): Shutterstock Images/Vadim Ratnikov; p. 65 (j): Shutterstock Images/Coprid; p. 65 (k): Shutterstock Images/John Kasawa; p. 66 (TL): Alamy/©jay goebel; p. 67 (CR): Alamy/©eye35.pix; p. 68 (TL): Alamy/©Bubbles Photolibrary; p. 69 (CR): Shutterstock Images/Minerva Studio; p. 70 (BC): Shutterstock Images/Pressmaster; p.70 (BR): Alamy/©PhotoAlto sas; p. 70 (TL): Alamy/©Jim West; p. 71 (TL): Alamy/©Purestock; p. 72 (TR): Alamy/©Justin Hannaford; p. 72 (CR): Alamy/©Chris Cooper-Smith; p. 72 (T): Shutterstock Images/CoolR; p. 72 (B): Shutterstock Images/Imagevixen; p. 73 (1): Alamy/©Cristina Fumi Photography; p. 73 (2): Shutterstock Images/Felix Rohan; p. 73 (3): Shutterstock Images/Alex Staroseltsev; p. 73 (4): Shutterstock Images/MNI; p. 73 (5): Shutterstock Images/Elena Blokhina; p. 73 (6): Shutterstock Images/Mama_mia; p. 74-75 (B/G): Corbis/Wave; p. 75 (a):Shutterstock Images/Lafoto; p. 75 (b): Shutterstock Images/st.djura; p. 75 (c): Shutterstock Images/Morten Normann Almeland; p. 75 (d): Shutterstock Images/Vaju Ariel; p. 75 (e): Shutterstock Images/Gts; p. 75 (f): Alamy/©Zacarias Pereira Da Mata; p. 75 (g): Shutterstock Images/chaoss; p. 75 (h): Shutterstock Images/jo Crebbin; p. 75 (i): Alamy/©Avico Ltd; p. 76 (TR): Alamy/©Keith J Smith; p. 77 (TR): Shutterstock Images/Sekar B; p. 78 (T): Alamy/©Paul Mayall Australia; p. 78 (a): Shutterstock Images/Gresei; p. 78 (b): Shutterstock Images/Brian A Jackson; p. 78 (c): Shutterstock Images/Nikitabuida; p. 78 (d): Alamy/©BSIP SA; p. 78 (e): Shutterstock Images/Tony740607; p. 78 (f): Shutterstock Images/Grynold; p. 78 (g): Shutterstock Images/Tatiana Popova; p. 78 (h): Shutterstock Images/Ti Santi; p. 78 (i): Alamy/©D.Hurst; p. 79 (TR): Getty Images/Nacivet; p. 80 (TL): Shutterstock Images/Lamreal-kobzeva; p. 80 (CL): Shutterstock Images/scyther5; p. 80 (BL): Shutterstock Images/Ervin Monn; p. 81 (TR): Alamy/©Blend Images; p. 82 (TR): Corbis/Jim Reed/Jim Reed Photography - Severe &; p. 82 (TL): Shutterstock Images/Minerva Studio; p. 82 (B/G): Shutterstock Images/Minerva Studio; p. 83 (BL): Shutterstock Images/Gorillaimages; p. 84-85 (B/G): Alamy/©Science Photo Library; p. 85 (CR): Alamy/©JGI/Jamie Grill/Blend Images; p. 86 (T): Shutterstock Images/Littleny; p. 87 (BR): Getty Images/Mark Bowden; p. 88 (a): Shutterstock Images/Syda Productions; p. 88 (b): Alamy/©Blend Images; p. 88 (c): Getty Images/Yellow Dog Productions; p. 88 (d): Getty Images/iStockphoto; p. 89 (CR): Getty Images/Debra Roets/Le Club Symphonie; p. 90 (TL): Shutterstock Images/Goodluz; p. 91 (TR): Shutterstock Images/Stephen Coburn; p. 92 (TL): Alamy/©Liquid Light; p. 92 (TL): Alamy/©Kathy deWitt; p. 92 (TL): Alamy/©Tim Graham; p. 92 (B): Shutterstock Images/FrameAngel; p. 94-95 (B/G): Corbis/Pete Saloutos/Image Source; p. 96 (TL): Alamy/©Arieliona; p. 97 (TR): Alamy/©Redsnapper; p. 98 (TL): Alamy/©Steve Lindridge; p. 99 (CR): Alamy/©Paul/F1online Digitale Bildagentur GmbH; p. 100 (TL): Alamy/©Robert Harding World Imagery; p. 100 (BL): Alamy/©Bob Daemmrich; p. 101 (TL): Alamy/©Steve Skjold; p. 102 (T, B/G): Alamy/©Zuma Press; p. 104-105 (B/G): Corbis/Marc Dozier; p. 120 (BR): Alamy/©The Print Collector; Back cover: Shutterstock Images/fluke samed.

Front cover photography by Alamy/©Martin Strmiska.

The publishers are grateful to the following illustrators:
Q2A Media Services, Inc. p. 6, 116, 120; Martin Sanders p. 28.

All video stills by kind permission of:
Discovery Communications, LLC 2015: p. 2 (1, 3, 4), 5, 10, 11, 12 (1, 3), 15, 20, 22 (1, 3, 4), 25, 30, 31, 32 (1, 3), 35, 40, 42 (1, 3, 4), 45, 50, 51, 54 (1, 3), 57, 62, 64 (1, 3, 4), 67, 72, 73, 74 (1, 3), 77, 82, 84 (1, 3, 4), 87, 92, 93, 94 (1, 3), 97, 102, 116, 117, 118, 119, 120; Cambridge University Press: p. 2 (2), 8, 12 (2), 18, 22 (2), 28, 32 (2), 38, 42 (2), 48, 54 (2), 60, 64 (2), 70, 74 (2), 80, 84 (2), 90, 94 (2), 100.

Credits

The authors and publishers acknowledge the following sources of copyright material and are grateful for the permissions granted. While every effort has been made, it has not always been possible to identify the sources of all the material used, or to trace all copyright holders. If any omissions are brought to our notice, we will be happy to include the appropriate acknowledgements on reprinting.

p. 2 (1): Shutterstock Images/Michael Wick; p. 2 (2): Shutterstock Images/Menno Schaefer; p. 2 (3): Shutterstock Images/Ragnisphoto; p. 10 (CR): Alamy/©Tetra Images; p. 21 (TL): Alamy/©Juice Images; p. 25 (TL): Alamy/©Keith Morris; p. 27 (TR): Getty Images/Manfred Rutz; p. 28 (BR): Alamy/©Maria Galan; p. 38 (CL): Getty images/Roy Mehta; p. 44 (1): Alamy/©Ruslan Kudrin; p. 44 (2): Shutterstock Images/Elena Elisseeva; p. 44 (3): Shutterstock Images/Gtstudio; p. 44 (4): Shutterstock Images/Quang Ho; p. 44 (5): Shutterstock Images/Sophie McAulay; p. 44 (6): Shutterstock Images/Coolkengzz; p. 44 (7): Alamy/©Paul Debois; p. 44 (8): Shutterstock Images/Yevgeniy11; p. 49 (TR): Shutterstock Images/Mila Supinskaya; p. 55 (TL): Alamy/©Acumen images; Back cover: Shutterstock Images Images/Fluke Samed.

Front cover photograph by Alamy/©Martin Strmiska.

The publishers are grateful to the following illustrators:
Janet Allinger p. 6, 8, 34, 40, 68; David Belmonte p. 4, 16, 17, 42, 43, 70; Galia Bernstein p. 18 (BR), 20, 23, 45, 46; Anni Betts p. 5, 37, 39, 66; Nigel Dobbyn p. 12, 26, 30, 33, 50, 54, 62; Mark Duffin p. 18 (1-10), 52; Q2A Media Services, Inc. p. 9, 11, 28, 50 (1, 2, 4, 5, 9), 56, 60, 61, 76; Jose Rubio p. 14, 31, 47, 48, 67.

All video stills by kind permission of Discovery Communications, LLC 2015.

Notes

Notes

Notes

Notes

Notes